Journal of Biblical Literature
Monograph Series, Volume III

THE PESHITTO

OF

SECOND SAMUEL

by

Donald M. C. Englert

Professor of Hebrew and Old Testament Science
The Theological Seminary, Lancaster, Pa.

Society of Biblical Literature and Exegesis
222 North Fifteenth Street
Philadelphia 2, Pennsylvania
1949

THE PESHITTO OF SECOND SAMUEL

Printed in the United States of America
on acid-free paper

∞

The present work is the third volume of the Monograph Series established by the Society of Biblical Literature in 1946. Professor Englert's study of the Peshitto Syriac version of the Second Book of Samuel was original-ly undertaken as a dissertation submitted for the degree of Doctor of Philosophy to the faculty of Dropsie College. In the opinion of the members of the Dropsie faculty and the editors of the Journal of Biblical Literature the dissertation is worthy of inclusion in the present se-ries.

For aid in the preparation of the work for publication thanks are due not only to those scholars mentioned in the conclusion to Professor Englert's Introduction but also to several scholars consulted by the editors, in particular to Dr. Joshua Bloch of the New York Public Library.

Ralph Marcus
Editor of the Monograph Series

TABLE OF CONTENTS

INTRODUCTION

IT IS REMARKABLE that to none of the ancient versions of the Bible has been paid as little attention as
to the Syriac, which, owing to its great antiquity, is
one of the most valuable documents in ascertaining the
original text of the Bible. In point of age, it takes
precedence of every other oriental text, excepting, of
course, the LXX.

The critical and exegetical value of the Peshitto is
now universally recognized. The study of its text,
therefore, deserves the attention of scholars. A
number of studies have appeared dealing with the text
of the books of the Syriac Old Testament, some of them
inadequately done. Of the recent literature on the
Peshitto, Haefeli[1] has written the most complete work.
Since Haefeli's study is in German and comparatively
inaccessible in this country, I have thought it advisable
to include a summary of his findings at this point.

Over a century ago, Hirzel[2] published the first
study of the Pentateuch in which he found that the
Peshitto followed the Hebrew text and Jewish exegesis
closely; he also noted that the Peshitto often agreed
with the Alexandrine version and the Samaritan Pentateuch.

Mager[3] characterized the Peshitto version of Joshua
as a good, reliable work. The differences from the MT

he attributed either to the translator's endeavor to make the translation flowing and intelligible, or to the corruption of MT, or to the translator's ignorance of geographical data. The Peshitto to Judges was studied by Lazarus[4] but his work is described by Haefeli[5] as simply an effort to explain the differences between the Syriac text and MT.

The books of I and II Kings were examined by Berlinger[6] and Barnes[7], respectively. I Kings was described by the former to be neither free nor slavishly literal. The latter's work was characterized by Haefeli[8] as confined to a study of the attestation of the text in printed editions and manuscripts. Of more value, perhaps, is Rosenwasser's work.[9]

Ruth was found by Janichs[10] to be very free and paraphrastic. Chronicles was studied by Barnes[11], whose work was described by Haefeli[12] as containing no statements as to the nature or condition of the text. Fränkel characterized the Peshitto to Chronicles as a purely Jewish Targum.[13] Esther was considered by Grünthal[14] as a word for word translation, true to the text and readable but not slavishly literal.

Job has been studied by Stenij[15], Mandl[16], and Baumann[17] and described as a faithful translation of the original. It has also been studied in great detail by Zimmerman, whose work is in manuscript form

but will probably appear in the near future. The
Peshitto Psalter has been the object of several studies:
by Barnes[18], Baethgen[19], and Berg?[20] They found that the
Syriac translator did not want a paraphrase but a word
for word translation, faithful to the original. At
the same time, it was evident that the liturgical and
religious purpose of the translation favored a free,
rather than a slavishly literal, translation.

Proverbs was the object of two studies: by Pinkuss[21]
and Chajes[22]. They describe it as rather free but faithful to the original. Besides the afore-mentioned work
of Janichs, Kamenetzky[23] also examined the Peshitto to
Koheleth and found it close to the MT but differing in
minor details. It followed Qere and was strongly influenced by the LXX. The translation of The Song of
Songs was characterized by Euringer[24] as faithful to
the original without being slavish. Salkind[25] concur-
red.

Isaiah claimed the attention of Diettrich[26] who
noted the independence of the Peshitto but in difficult
passages its dependence on LXX. It, too, followed Qere.
The book of Jeremiah was examined by Frankl who found
that it follows the Alexandrine version and the Targum
of Jonathan.[27] Cornill on Ezekiel found it a free translation; the translator wanted to give the sense of the

original without following it slavishly.[28]

The minor prophets were studied by Credner[29] and Sebök[30], who characterized the translator as motivated by a desire to give the sense of the original without being too literal. Lamentations, examined by Abalesz[31], was described as true to the MT. Ezra was studied by Hawley[32] and characterized as carefully made and true to the sense without being slavishly literal. Wyngaarden, I have been told, has worked on Daniel. Nehemiah was the subject of R.L. Harris' unpublished thesis.

In 1897, Emanuel Schwartz published his work on I Samuel.[33] His method, on the whole superficial, was to go through the book verse by verse, listing the MT, LXX, and Peshitto, together with the Targum when it had a bearing on the case. Listing ten pages of examples, he came to the conclusion that "the Syriac translator had before him a Hebrew text which in all essentials corresponds to our present text but that this text differed from our present text in single instances of a subordinate nature."[34]

Because Schwartz studied only I Samuel and that not too well, it was my desire to examine the companion volume of II Samuel, hoping some day to rework I Samuel in a more satisfactory form. The MT which was used

was P.Kahle's revised edition of R. Kittel's third
edition of Biblia Hebraica (Stuttgart, 1937). Those
cases in which the Peshitto and LXX agree over against
MT were recorded, as well as those in which the Peshitto goes its own way over against MT and LXX.

This study begins with the study of the transmission
of the Peshitto text. Of the representative texts
used, it is apparent that the Ambrosian manuscript is
the most valuable aid to the text critic of the Old
Testament. Then the treatment of the MT by Peshitto
is studied. Here it is seen that the Peshitto, while
not slavishly literal, gives the sense of the original
fairly well, while feeling free to paraphrase from time
to time. The important question of the relation of the
Peshitto to the LXX and other ancient versions is taken
up next. An appendix shows that the Syriac of II
Samuel was emended to agree with its parallel in Psalm
18.

Finally, I wish to acknowledge my deep gratitude to
Solomon L. Skoss, who, with the late James A. Mont-
gomery, gave me my introduction to Syriac studies, and
especially to Joseph Reider, whose guidance and un-
failing patience aided me immeasureably in the preparation of this study. This book is dedicated to Sarah,
without whose inspiration it would not have been done.

Notes

1. L. Haefeli "Die Peschitta des Alten Testamentes mit
    Rücksicht auf ihre textkritiscke Bearbeitung und
    Herausgabe" in <u>Alttestamentliche Abhandlungen</u> XI
    (Münster, 1927), 23 ff.

2. L. Hirzel <u>De Pentateuchi Versionis Syriacae</u>, <u>quam
    Peschitto</u> <u>vocant</u>, <u>indole</u> (Lipsiae, 1825), p. 102.

3. H. Mager <u>Die Peschittho zum Buch Josua</u> (Freiburg,
    1916) p. 111.

4. A. Lazarus <u>Zur syrischen Übersetzung des Buches der
    Richter</u> (Kirchhain N.-L., 1901), pp. 32-71.

5. Haefeli, <u>op</u>. <u>cit</u>., 26 "Er stellt sich bloss die
    Aufgabe, die Abweichungen des Syrers vom massore-
    tischen Text, soweit immer möglich, zu erklären."

6. J. Berlinger, <u>Die Peschitta zum 1</u>. (<u>3</u>.) <u>Buch der
    Könige und ihr Verhältnis zur MT</u>, <u>LXX</u>, <u>und Trg</u>.
    (Berlin, 1897).

7. W.Barnes "The Peschitta Version of 2 Kings" in <u>JTS</u>,
    VI (1904-1905), 220 ff.

8. Haefeli, <u>op</u>. <u>cit</u>. p. 27, "Sie (seine Arbeit) bezieht
    sich weniger auf den Text als solchen als auf seine
    Bezeugung in Drucken und Handschriften."

9. Rosenwasser <u>Der Lexikalische Stoff der Königbücher
    der Peschitta</u> (Berlin, 1905).

10. G.Janichs <u>Animadversiones criticae in versionem
    syriacam Peschitthonianam librorum Koheleth et Ruth</u>

Notes

(Lipsiae, 1869), p. 34.

11. W. Barnes _An Apparatus Criticus to Chronicles in the Peschitta Version with a discussion of the value of the Codex Ambrosianus_ (Cambridge, 1897).

12. Haefeli, _op. cit_, 28-29 "Sie (seine Arbeit) enthält keinerlei Angaben über die Textbeschaffenheit der Chronik."

13. Frankel "Die Syrische Übersetzung zu den Büchern der Chronik" in _Jahrbuch für Protestantische Theologie_, V (1897), 508 ff. and 720 ff.

14. J. Grünthal _Die Syrische Übersetzung zum Buche Esther_ (Breslau, 1900), pp. 21-55.

15. E. Stenij, _Dissertatio de Syriaca libri Jobi interpretatione, quae Peshita vocatur_ (Helsingforsiae, 1887)

16. A. Mandl _Die Peschitta zu Hiob_ (Leipzig und Budapest, 1892)

17. Baumann, "Die Verwendbarkeit der Peschita zum Buche Job für die Textkritik" in _ZAW_, XVII(1898), 508 ff. and XIX, 15 ff.

18. W. Barnes _The Peschitta Psalter according to the West Syrian Text, edited with an apparatus criticus_ (Cambridge, 1904)

19. F. Baethgen _Untersuchungen über die Psalmen nach der Peschitta_ (Kiel, 1878)

Notes

20. J.F. Berg The Influence of the Septuagint upon the Peschitta Psalter (New York, 1895), p. 13 ff.

21. Pinkuss "Die Syrische Übersetzung der Proverbien textkritisch und in ihrem Verhältnisse zu dem massoretischen Text, den Septuagint, und dem Targum untersucht" in ZAW, XIV (1894), 65-141.

22. Chajes "Etwas über die Peschitta zu den Proverbien" in JQR, XIII (1901) 86 ff.

23. Kamenetzky "Die Peschitta zu Koheleth textkritisch und in ihr Verhältnis zu dem massoretischen Text, der Septuaginta, und den andren alten griechischen Versionen" in ZAW, XXIV (1904) 181-239.

24. Seb. Euringer "Die Bedeutung der Peschitto für die Textkritik des Hohenliedes" in Biblische Studien, VI (1901), 117-128.

25. J.M.Salkind Die Peschitta zu Schir-Haschirim text-kritisch und in ihrem Verhältnis zu MT, und LXX untersucht (Leiden, 1905).

26. Diettrich "Apparatus criticus zur Peschitta zum Propheten Jesaia" in Beihefte zur ZAW, VIII (1905).

27. P.F.Frankl Studien über die Septuaginta und Peschito zu Jeremia (Breslau, 1873).

28. C. Cornill Das Buch des Propheten Ezechiel (Leipzig 1886), p. 137 ff.

Notes

29. C.A. Credner De prophetarum minorum versionis
     syriacae quam Peschitto dicunt indole (Gottingae,
     1827), pp. 82-112.

30. M. Sebök Die Syrische Übersetzung der 12 kleinen
     Propheten und ihr Verhältnis zu dem massoretischen
     Text und zu den älteren Übersetzungen namentlich
     den LXX und den Targum (Leipzig, 1887), pp. 1-9.

31. A. Abalesz, Die Syrische Übersetzung der Klage-
     lieder und ihr Verhältnis zu Targum und LXX
     (Privigye, 1895), p. 41 ff.

32. C.A. Hawley A Critical Examination of the Peshitta
     Version of the Book of Ezra (New York, 1922), p.10.

33. F. Schwartz Die Syrische Übersetzung des ersten
     Buches Samuelis und ihr Verhältnis zu MT, LXX, und
     Trg. (Berlin, 1897).

34. Schwartz, ibid., p. 93.

Chapter I

TRANSMISSION OF THE PESHITTO TEXT

THE EDITIO PRINCEPS of the Peshitto is that in the
Paris Polyglot (1629-1645). Unfortunately, this was
based on a manuscript written only a few years before
and was probably the poorest one available to the editor, Gabriel Sionita, at the time. This was reproduced
without improvement in the London Polyglot by Brian
Walton in 1657. This we have designated as P^L. In
1823, Samuel Lee published the London Polyglot Peshitto
in a separate edition with minor changes. This we shall
call P^{Le}.

In 1852 Rev. Justin Perkins, an American missionary,
issued a new edition of the Peshitto, printed in Urmia,
Persia. It was not available to me, nor was its absence
from this study considered unduly important. G.F.Moore
has written, "On the whole the text of the Urmia Bible
is distinctly inferior to that of Lee and the Polyglots."
The edition of the Peshitto published by the Dominicans
of Mosul in 1887-91 contains both the Old and New Testaments. Its existence is comparatively unknown. This,
however, may be due to the fact that its value for the
textual critic is very small, if any whatever. We shall
call this P^M. The witness of Bar Hebraeus and Ephraem
Syrus, when pertinent, was also used. They will be

designated p^{BH} and p^{ES}, respectively.

By far the most important text of the Peshitto is that of a sixth century codex in the Ambrosian Library in Milan, edited in photolithographic form by A.M. Ceriani (Translatio Syra Peschitto Veteris Testamenti ex codice Ambrosiano sec. fere VI, photolithographice edita curante et adnotante Sac. Ob. Antonia Maria Ceriani, (Mediolani, 1873-1883). This we have designated as p^A.

In spite of the unfavorable opinion of Cornill[2], this manuscript seems to be, all things considered, certainly the most valuable authority we possess for the Peshitto text of the Old Testament. Cornill's conclusion that "of all the accessible texts of the Peshitta, A was the worst", he subsequently changed in a private letter to Barnes[3] due to Rahlfs' article "Beiträge zur Textkritik ler Peschita" in ZATW, (1889) 161-210.[4]

p^A was compared to $p^{L,Le,M}$ and found to be definitely superior to them. They omitted words found in MT, LXX, V, and T. They also added words not found in the ancient versions. In several cases, the translation found in p^A represented the original text supported by the versions. In several cases, $p^{L,Le,M}$ seem to represent the original text of MT but, here too, the difference in p^A can be explained as the confusion of letters which look alike.

$P^{L,Le}$ omitted:

10:18 (P^{M} also) ܐܪܡ

13:3 ܘܡܛܠܗ

19:41 (MT v. 42) ܛܠܡܐ

21:4 ܐܢܫ

21:5 ܟܠܐ

$P^{L,Le}$ added:

10:15 ܒܢ̈ܝ

11:1 ܠܩܪܒܐ

13:28 ܘ to ܠܐ ܬܕܚܠܘܢ

17:10 (also P^{M}) changing meaning ܠܐ

20:22 ܕܘܡ

23:18 ܘܗܘ ܗܘܐ ܪܝܫܐ ܕܬܠܬܝܢ

P^{A} represents the original text, supported by the Versions:

12:4 $P^{A,M}$ ܠܐܪܚܐ ܕܐܬܐ ܠܗ so MT, LXX, V, T.
$P^{L,Le}$ ܠܐܪܚܐ ܕܥܠܗ

15:7 P^{A} ܚܒܪܢ so MT, T.
$P^{L,Le,M,BH,ES.}$ ܚܒܪ̈ܢ so LXX, V.

20:14 $P^{A,M,BH}$ ܒܪ̈ܝܡ so MT,V,T.
$P^{L,Le}$ ܟܪ̈ܝܡ so LXX.

22:34 $P^{A,M}$ ܪܘܡ so MT,V.
$P^{L,Le}$ ܪܘܡܐ so LXX

22:36 P^{A} ܕܦܘܪܩܢܟ so MT,V,T.
$P^{L,Le,M}$ ܕܦܘܪܩܢܐ so LXX

23:28 $P^{A,M,BH}$ ܕܡ ܢܛܘܦܬ so MT, LXX^{B},V. T.

pL,Le ܐܝܟ ܗܘܐ

There are a few cases in which P^A and P^{L,Le,M} differ, yet neither can be said to have the reading which is better:

    2:24   P^{A,M}+ ܘ ܘܡܗ   pL,Le + ܘ ܘܡܒܐ

    11:4   P^{A,M}+ ܗܒܐ ܘ ܓܠ

                pL,Le+ ܗܒܐ ܝ ܓܠ

    13:39 MT ܠ ܒ ܐܖ   P^A ܘ ܗܡܒܠܐ

                pL,Le,M   ܘ ܠܠܐܠܐ

    14:7 MT ܐܘܫܝ P^{A,Le} ܝ ܗܒܡܚ

              pL,M   ܝ ܗܒܡܚ

    15:32 P^A ܐ ܙܒܠ   pL,Le,M   ܙܒܠ

           perhaps haplography due to preceding word ܘܪܚܒܐ

    16:10 P^A ܘܡܒܡܚ ܝ   pL,Le,M ܘܝ ܗܡܒܡܘ

    19:13 (P v.12) P^A+ ܘܒܠ ܘܗ ܙܒܛܐܘ

          pL,Le,M   ܘܒܠ ܘܗ ܛܠܒܐ ܙܒܛܐܘ

    22:36 MT ܘܝܪܛ ܐ P^{A,M} ܗܒܩܒܗ

          pL,Le   ܘܒܩܒܐܠ ܓ

    23:35 MT ܦܪܟ P^A ܘܗ

          pL,Le   ܘ ܢܟ   p^M ܘ ܢ

In order to ascertain the relative value of p^{L,Le,M} over against P^A, let us examine those cases in which they seem to have the better reading:

    2:16 P^{A,BH} ܓܐ ܀   so LXX

          pL,Le,M   ܓܐ ܀   so MT. But this can be

explained as inner Syriac Corruption and

confusion of) and ;

13:19 p^L,BH |ܐܕܠܝܒ so MT, LXX, V, T.

p^A,Le,M |ܐܕܠܝܒ but there is no such word.

This error was due to the confusion between

ܒ and ܒ

13:20 p^L,M ܟܠܟ so MT, LXX, V, T.

p^A,Le ܟܠܟ but there is no such word.

This error was due to the confusion of ܒ

and ܒ

19:17 (P v. 16) p^A > ܟܚܛܒ ܒܪܝ This omission by

p^A cannot be satisfactorily explained and

must therefore be counted over against the

5 omissions by p^L,Le.

19:36 (P v. 35) p^L,Le |ܠܝ ܪܡܘ |ܪ ܡܝ

MT שָׁרִים (שָׁרוֹת MT) p^A |ܠ ܪܡܠܘ |ܡܝ

p^M |ܚܐܡܒܒܘ ܦܝܢܒܒ To my mind,

p^A in its present form must go back to

|ܕܝ ܡܘ ܦܝܡ of which its present form is

a corruption. p^L,Le represent a reading of

MT as שָׁרִים ושָׁרוֹת

From the fact that p^L,Le make omissions from and

additions to the text (such omissions and additions

being supported nowhere in the other ancient versions);

and that p^A, on the other hand, in several cases re-

presents the original text, supported in the other
ancient versions, we can venture the opinion that of
the four representative texts of the Peshitto to II
Samuel which were used, P^A is definitely the best .

Inner Syriac Corruptions

Besides this comparison of the four representative
texts of the Peshitto, it is important to learn how
well the Peshitto was transmitted through the centuries.
How many Syriac errors crept into the text by the confusion of letters which looked alike?

There are a number of cases in which the differences
between MT and P would lead one to suppose that the
translator had before him a text which differed from our
present MT. However, upon closer examination, it will
be seen that the differences are due to inner Syriac
errors. This can be attributed to the confusion between ܠ and ܡ, ܀ and ܝ, ܝ and ܟ, ܡ and ܣ, ܐ and ܒ,
ܒ and ܟ, ܀ and ܝ, ܀ and ܝ, ܀ and ܐ, ܕ and ܞ .
Metathesis also explains several of these differences.

    I. Confusion of ܠ and ܐ

       2:24 ܢܒܠ which is a corruption of ܐܒܠ, so

          MT, LXX, T.[5] V aquae ductus.

    II. Confusion of ܒ and ܒ

       23:32 ܠܠܢܚܝ, a corruption of ܠܠܒܚܝ, so

MT, LXX[A], V.T.[6]

III. Confusion of ܓ and ܟ

18:17 ܟܘܡܚ , a corruption of ܚܕܚܟ , so
MT,LXX,V,T.

23:20 ܟܚܕ a corruption of ܓܘܚ , so MT,LXX,
V.T. This confusion may not be orthographic but
represents perhaps a phonetic confusion since
the strong 'Ain in Semitic in general has a sound
approximating Gimel.

IV. Confusion of ܙ and ܪ

19:10 (P 9) ܙܬ a corruption of ܪܬ , so
MT,LXX,V.T.

23:5 ܪܡܗܩ, a corruption of ܟܙܘܩ , so
MT,LXX,V.T. Metathesis also occurred.

V. Confusion of ܡ and ܣ , also ܥ

18:29 p[A,L] ܙܡܪ , a corruption of ܪܡܪ, so
MT,LXX, V.T. p[Le] ܙܣܪ

VI. Confusion of ܣ and ܒ

3:7 and 21:8 ܒܐ , a corruption of ܣܐ , so
MT,LXX,V,T.[7]

5:15 ܒܩܫ , a corruption of ܣܩܫ , so MT,LXX,V,T
12:8 ܩܨܒ a corruption of ܣܘܒ , so MT,LXX,V,T.
23:36 ܣܠ ܒܠ a corruption of ܣܠܒ , so MT,
LXX,V,T.

VII. Confusion of ܣ and ܒ , as well as ܪ and ܙ
11:21 ܪܘܣܚܠ , a corruption of ܚܠܙܘ, so

MT,LXX,V,T.

VIII.Confusion of ܒ and ܟ

    12:21 ܘܟܒܠ , a corruption of ܘܒܚܠ , so

MT,LXX,V,T.

IX. Confusion of ܖ and ܪ

    20:26 p^A ܒܪ ܐ p^L,Le ܒܪ ܐ , a corruption

of ܒܪܙ ܐ , so MT, LXX,V,T.

X. Confusion of ܖ and ܙ

    17:13 ܙܖܙ ܐ a corruption of ܙܪܕ ܐ , so MT,

LXX,V,T.

XI. Confusion of ܖ and ܗ

    2:30 ܡܚܣܪ ܙ ܠ, a corruption of ܡܚܣܪ ܐ ܠ, so

MT,LXX,V,T.

XII.Confusion of ܠ and ܥ

    4:6 ܡܠܦ , a corruption of ܡܦܠܥ ܐ, so MT,

LXX,V,T.

XIII. Metathesis explains:

    3:27 ܘܒܣܝܗ , a corruption of ܘܒܫܦܗ , so

MT,LXX,V,T. Besides metathesis, phonetic con-

fusion of ܥ and ܣ took place.

    13:4 ܐܪܠܐ , a corruption of ܪܐܠܐ , so MT,LXX,V,T.

    17:27 ܐܚܣܒܠ , a corruption of ܚܣܥ , so MT,

LXX,V,T.

As might be anticipated from the nature of the

characters of the Syriac alphabet, the Peshitto of II

Samuel exhibits some inner Syriac corruption, of which perhaps there may be more examples than those noted above. It is almost impossible to detect all of them in the course of such a study.

Driver[8] makes the observation on the state of the text of both books of Samuel that "the Syriac text of Peshitto sometimes exhibits corruptions similar to those noticed in the case of LXX" and records several examples of such inner Syriac corruption in I and II Samuel. Others have made similar observations.[9]

When one considers the numerous similarities in the characters of the Syriac alphabet and when one remembers the circumstances under which the manuscripts were transmitted, it is surprising, not that errors in transmission crept into the text, but rather that there are not more of them.

Thus we can say that the Peshitto to II Samuel has been comparatively well preserved and has come down to us relatively free from textual corruption.

Notes

1. Andover Review, VII (January, 1887), 101.

2. Cornill, op. cit., p. 145

3. Barnes, op. cit., p. x.

4. Ibid., pp. xxii-xxiii.

5. Lagarde, Onomastica Sacra (Göttingen, 1887), 37,5; 97,6 as Amma; 226,31 as "Ἀρα

6. Ibid., 38,14 as Eliaba

7. Ibid., 37,8 as Aia

8. Driver, Notes on the Hebrew Text and the Topography of the Books of Samuel (Oxford, 1913), p. lxxv.

9. Haefeli, op. cit., p. 25

Chapter II
TREATMENT OF THE MASSORETIC TEXT

A TRANSLATION OF a piece of literature can take one
of many forms. It can be slavishly literal as was
Aquila's translation of the OT. On the other hand, it
can be a paraphrase, barely approximating the original,
as are some of the Targums. Between these extremes of
literalness and freedom are many possible shades of
difference.

At times, the Peshitto takes on the characteristics
of both extremes. In some cases, the Hebrew idiom is
reproduced exactly, while in others the utmost freedom
of expression is found. For the most part, however, it
can be said that the Peshitto to II Samuel belongs
more to the school of freedom than to the extreme of
literalness. As is to be found in other ancient versions, the tendency to be free occurs more frequently
in difficult passages which do not lend themselves to
a clear understanding of their meaning.

The examples of literal translation in the Peshitto
of II Samuel are too numerous to cite. A few examples
from chapter 1 will suffice:

1:2 MT	וַיְהִי בַּיּוֹם הַשְּׁלִישִׁי וְהִנֵּה אִישׁ בָּא
	מִן הַמַּחֲנֶה מֵעִם שָׁאוּל וּבְגָדָיו
	קְרֻעִים וַאֲדָמָה עַל רֹאשׁוֹ

P   [Syriac text]

1:3 MT   וַיֹּאמֶר לֹו דָּוִד אֵי מִזֶּה תָּבֹוא
וַיֹּאמֶר אֵלָיו מִמַּחֲנֵה יִשְׂרָאֵל נִמְלָטְתִּי

P   [Syriac text]

1:7 MT   וַיִּפֶן אַחֲרָיו וַיִּרְאֵנִי וַיִּקְרָא אֵלָי
וָאֹמַר הִנֵּנִי

P   [Syriac text]

1:8 MT   וַיֹּאמֶר לִי מִי־אָתָּה וַיֹּאמֶר אֵלָיו
עֲמָלֵקִי אָנֹכִי

P   [Syriac text]

1:9 MT   וַיֹּאמֶר אֵלַי עֲמָד־נָא עָלַי וּמֹתְתֵנִי
כִּי אֲחָזַנִי הַשָּׁבָץ כִּי־כָל־עֹוד נַפְשִׁי בִּי

P   [Syriac text]

Other examples of literal translation can be seen in
1:10, 1:11, 1:13, 14,15,16,17,18,20,22,23,25,26,27.

   P's free handling of MT is shown in the following
ways:

   I.   P misread MT:

     7:23 MT   וְזַרְאֹות , so LXX,V,T. But P

   [Syriac text] reading וְזַרְאֹות

8:13   MT שֻׁ ם , so LXX,V. But P ܠܛ

reading שֻׁם

10:4   MT בַּחֲצִ֥י so LXX,V,T. But P ܟܦܠܝ̈ܪܐ

reading חֲ ם וְ

13:9   MT וַתֵּ֣צ֥ק so LXX,V,T. But P ܘܣܡܬ

reading וַתֵּ֣צ֥ג

14:17   MT לִמְנֻחָ֖ה so LXX,V,T. But P ܗܡܙܟܡ

reading לִמְנֻחָ֖ה

14:24   MT וּפָנַ֣י לֹ֥א יִרְאֶ֑ה   so LXX,V,T.

But P ܘܐܦ̈ܘܗܝ ܠܐ ܢܚܙܐ reading וּפָנַ֣י

17:9   MT הַשְּׁפָ֑עֵ so LXX,V,T. But P ܠܟܠ

reading הַשְׁפַ֑ע

20:8   MT בַּתַּבְרָה so LXX,V,T. But P ܘܐܣܪ ܠܗ

reading ךְּ for בְ

20:19   MT שְׁלֻמֵ֣י so LXX,V,T. But P ܐܠ ܦܙ

reading שְׁלֻמֵ֣י

20:19   MT צִ֥יר so LXX,V,T. But P ܟܠܗ

reading וָצֵ֥ר

22:46   MT טָפָּסְגְּר֣וֹת ם   so LXX,V,T.

But P ܡܚܬܟܘ ܘ reading טָפָּגְר֣וֹת ם

23:1   MT עַל but P ܡܙܪ| reading עָ֥ל

II. P added words to MT:

The following ameliorative additions were made:

3:29   MT וְאֶל כָּל בֵּ֥ית P ܟܠܗ ܒܝܬ ܘܠܟܠܗ

8:18   MT וְהַכְּרֵתִ֥י   P added ܓܒܪ̈ܐ so V,T.

12:25 סרמר implying יְדַוְ in explanation of

יְדִיהָ

12:30 MT וַאֶבֶן P prefaces ܚܘܣܐ ܠܘ so V,T.,

parallel in I Chron. 20:2.

23:3 MT וַאֶרֶת P adds ܒ so 20 Mss.,V,T.

Proper names were added:

2:3; 11:7; 14:1; 16:5; 16:10; 24:20 and twice in

24:23   ܝܘܣ

6:18; 14:11; 18:29; 19:20 (P v. 19); 19:27

(P.v. 26); 19:37 (P. v. 36) ܝܙܛ

8:10 ܘܣܠ ܚ ܒ ܘܣ

10:11 ܝܣܗܐ ܐ ܚܣܐ

11:7   ܝܛ ܘ ܚ

11:19 and 20:22   ܘ ܐ ܒ

12:9   ܝܛܒ ܩܬ ܩ

13:4   ܩܒ ܒ ܐ ܩ

14:33 and 18:9 ܒ ܘ ܚ ܒ

16:3   ܝ ܘ ܠ ܠ

19:25 (P v. 24) ܩ ܚ ܘ ܩ ܝ pES, LXX[A] follow MT

24:14   ܝ ܘ ܠ ܠ

Common nouns were added:

3:31 ܝ ܘ ܚ ܠ ܘ after וְדָוִד וְהַמֶּלֶךְ

5:1; 20:5; 24:25   ܒ ܠ

6:5   וָנוֹ

7:6	ܐܙܠܬ
7:10	ܣܡܠܬ
7:20	ܝܕܥܬ
7:26	ܫܠܝܛ ܛܪܒ ²º
9:11	ܛܡܣܠ
10:18	ܘܛܣܕ ܐܝܪܚܣ
10:19; 15:16	ܚܩܒ
11:11	ܐܛܪܙ ܐܥ ܪܕܪ
11:27	ܩܒܠܐ
14:11	ܪܙ ܚܪܘ
14:11, 12; 15:12; 19:25 (P v. 24)	ܛܠܒܛ
14:30	ܢܩܫܠܐ ܐܘ
14:33	ܛܠܒܛ ܂ܪܚܣܠܐܘ ܂ܛܒܠܐܘܡ
16:7,8	ܐ ܡܪ
17:8; 23:24; 24:9	ܐܪܚܒܠ
19:31 (P v. 30)	ܐܪܚܒ
19:38 (P v. 37); 23:30; 23:31	ܚܪ
19:42 (P v. 41)	ܚܩܒ ܂ܘܡܠܚܠ ܂
19:43 (P v. 42)	ܛܠܒ ܪ
20:18	ܐܬܠܬ
21:4	ܣܝܒ
21:12	ܚܠܩ ܪܙܐ
23:10	ܛ ܛܣܐ ܚ and ܐܬܠܩܡ
23:12	ܚ ܪܡ ܂ܘ and ܐܬܣܝܩ
23:30	ܛ ܪܚܣܝܒ

Appellatives were added:

7:4,17; 24:13; 24:14;
Adjectives were added:

3:20; 18:9,17; 23:
19:44 (P v. 43)

Prepositions were added:

5:2; 11:20; 19:11 (P v.10)
19:43 (P v. 42)

20:15 P+ to

**Conjunctions, interjections,
etc. were added:**

14:10; 19:19 (P v. 18)

19:40 (P v. 39); 24:10, 13
Verbs were added:

2:24 P^A

    pL, Le

2:30 , and

11:4 P^A

    pL, Le   19:11 (P v. 10)   ....

12:8   and   ....

         19:13 (P v. 12)

14:3   19:18 (P v. 17)

14:7   so V. T.   19:38 (P v. 37)

15:12   and   20:2

16:1   and   20:12   and

17:22   and

23:14 / مر · · · · مر ܙ

23:15 ܠܠ ܘ ܣ ܩܕ ܂

24:14   ܒܬ

24:16   ܩ ܩ

24:17 ܒܬ · · · · ܠܕ ܘܠ ܠܗܠ ܩ

Besides these cases, there are 31 examples of additions which P made to MT, following LXX, which are
dealt with in a subsequent chapter.

III. P omits portions of MT:

The omission of words, phrases, and clauses in
a translation may be due to several causes: homoioteleuton, a desire for improvement, and paraphrasing.

All those who find it necessary to do a great
deal of transcribing know by experience the omissions
which are due to what is technically called homoioteleuton; that is, when the clause ends with the same word
as closes a preceding sentence or clause. The trans-
criber's eye in such a case frequently wanders from
one word to the other, and causes him to omit the passag
which lies between them. The same effect is produced
when two or more sentences begin with the same words.

Homoioteleuton explains the following omissions
    by P:

13:18 The whole verse was omitted because both

v. 17 and v. 18 end with אָמַר וֹּ

14:15,16 P omits אֵת דְּבַר הַמֶּלֶךְ הַמֶּלֶךְ אֲלַי אָשֶׁר כִּי : וַהָפַן אֵלָי כִּי יִשְׁמַע הַמֶּלֶךְ

the eye of the translator having skipped

from אֶל־הַמֶּלֶךְ in vs. 15 to הַמֶּלֶךְ

in v. 16.

15:24 P omits וַיַּצִּקוּ אֵת־אֲרוֹן הָאֱלֹהִים

the eye having skipped from one הָאֱלֹהִים

to the other

15:30 P omits (וְהוּא הֹלֵךְ וְעָלֹה) probably because

of the similarity of עָלֹה to the preceding

הֹלֵךְ.

18:2,3 P omits גַּם־אֲנִי עִמָּכֶם :

וַיֹּאמֶר הָעָם לֹא תֵצֵא

probably because of the resemblance of אֵצֵא

to תֵצֵא

18:3 P omits וְאִם־יָמֻתוּ חֶצְיֵנוּ לֹא־יָשִׂימוּ אֵלֵינוּ לֵב

the eye having skipped from לֵב to לֵב

19:12 P omits וְהַמֶּלֶךְ דָּוִד שָׁלַח אֶל־צָדוֹק

וְאֶל־אֶבְיָתָר הַכֹּהֲנִים לֵאמֹר דַּבְּרוּ

אֶל־זִקְנֵי יְהוּדָה לֵאמֹר לָמָּה תִהְיוּ

אַחֲרֹנִים לְהָשִׁיב אֶת־הַמֶּלֶךְ

the eye having skipped from אֶת־הַמֶּלֶךְ

the last word of v. 11, to אֶת־הַמֶּלֶךְ

in v. 12.

23:25   P omits אֶל־אַ הַחֲתַרְדִּי   the eye having

　　　　skipped from הַחֲתַרְדִּי to הַחֲתַרְדִּי

24:6   The whole verse was omitted because v. 6 and

　　　　v. 7 begin with (וַיָּבֹאוּ

P makes ameliorative omissions:

2:31   (נֹתַ) so LXX[L]

3:12   וָתַחַן)

3:13   בְּבוֹאֲךָ לְרָאוֹת אֶת־פָּנַי

8:14   MT   וַיָּשִׁ֧ם בָּאֱדוֹם נְצִבִים בְּכָל־אֱדוֹם

　　　　שָׂ֥ם נְצִבִים

P.　　ܘܐܘܩܡ ܪ̈ܘܪܒܢܐ ܡܛܠ ܐܕܘܡ

making 1 phrase of 2

13:8   MT.   וַתֹּאמֶר חָמָס אֶת־הָרָעָה הַגְּדוֹלָה וַיְשַׁלְּחֵנִי

　　　　לְצֵאת וַיַּעַזְבֵנִי אֶת־הַדְּבָרִים

　　　　P.　ܘܝܗܒܢ ܝܬܝܪ ܕܫܕܪ ܠܟܘܢ

Omissions by P which change meaning:

1:21   בְּלִי

Proper names were omitted:

3:14	מִיכָל	16:6	מִמִּשְׁפַּחַת דָּוִד
5:9	בֶּן הַגָּלְעָדִי	20:1	יִשְׂרָאֵל
5:19	פְּלִשְׁתִּים	23:24	אֶלְחָנָן בֶּן דֹּדוֹ
9:5; 17:21	דָּוִד		בֵּית־לָחֶם
9:9	צֶר שָׁאוּל	24:11	חֹזֵה דָּוִד
13:29	לְאַמְנוֹן	24:21	אֲרַוְנָ

Common nouns were omitted:

2:3	עָרֵי	15:11	קְרֻאִים
2:23	הַחֲנִית ²⁰	15:18	שֵׁשׁ מֵאוֹת אִישׁ
3:38	אֶל-עֲבָדָיו	15:20	עִמָּךְ חֶסֶד וֶאֱמֶת
6:12 (so V); 6:15; 19:18		15:30; 16:18 (so V);	
(P v. 17) בֵּית		17:14,24; 18:20; 19:42	
6:17	בְּמְקוֹמוֹ	(P v. 41) אִישׁ	
7:6	וּבְמִשְׁכָּן	16:3	אֶל-הַמֶּלֶךְ
10:19	הַמְּלָכִים	17:11	כַּחוֹל אֲשֶׁר-עַל
11:2	מֵעַל הַגָּג		הַיָּם לָרֹב
11:13	בְּמִשְׁכָּבוֹ	17:13	אֶל-הָעִיר הַהִיא
11:21	עֵץ	18:6	בְּיַעַר אֶפְרָיִם
11:24	אֶל-עֲבָדֶךָ	18:7	בְּיוֹם הַהוּא
12:31	וּבְמַגְזְרֹת הַבַּרְזֶל	19:1 (P 18:33)	וַיֶּעְשׁר
13:7	הַבַּיְתָה	19:3 (P v. 2)	הִתְעַצֵּבוּ
13:16	מֵאַחֶרֶת	19:5 (P v. 4) (so LXX^L,	
13:22	דָּבָר אֲשֶׁר	V); 19:42 (P v. 41)	
13:25	הַמֶּלֶךְ אֶל-אַבְשָׁלוֹם	הַמֶּלֶךְ	
13:32	הַנְּעָרִים	19:6 (P v. 5)	הַבַּיְת
13:34	הַנַּעַר	19:7 (P v. 6)	וְיו ³⁰
14:12	אֲדֹנִי	19:17 (P v. 16)	
14:13	הַדָּבָר הַזֶּה	מִבַּחוּרִים	
14:15	אֲשֶׁר-בָּאתִי	19:18 (P v. 17) וְאֶלֶף	
14:26	בְּקֵץ	אִישׁ עִמּוֹ מִבִּנְיָמִן	
14:28	יָמִים	19:27 (P v. 26)	עַבְדְּךָ

19:35 (P v. 34) יְמֵי

19:44 (P v. 43) דִּבְרֵי

20:8 וַיָּצֻא חָגֹור

20:17 הָאִשָּׁה

20:21 הַדָּבָר

21:6 בְּחִיר יהוה

24:12 אַחַת מֵהֶם

24:15 מִן הָעָם ,

24:22 הָעֵצִים בְּעֵינֶךָ

Adjectives and adverbs were omitted:

3:1 אֲשֶׁר לֹה

4:11 צַדִּיק

7:1 מֵרִיב

7:22; 14:25; 18:8; 22:1

כֵּן

12:5; 13:15 מְאֹד

13:1 יָפֶה

17:18 מֵרַעֲה

18:10 אֶחָד

23:10 גְּדוּלָה

Prepositions were omitted:

3:16 אֵת הָ

12:17 עָלָיו

13:34 אַחֲרֵי

14:3 בְּדֶרֶךְ in בְּ

15:36 שָׁם ם

Conjunctions, interjections, etc. were omitted:

7:2 אָז

9:4; 13:24; 16:4; 16:5;

18:10 הֵןוֹ

12:5 אַף

12:6 עַל אֲשֶׁר

14:32 וְזֶהּ

15:21; 18:8 שָׁם

17:5 גַּם

17:13 עַד אֲשֶׁר

18:3 עַתָּה

19:7 twice and 19:21 כִּי

20:19 לָמָּה

21:17 עוֹד

Verbs were omitted:

1:5 יֵלֶךְ

1:5,6 הִגִּיד לֹו

2:23 וַיָּמָת

3:13,18 לֵאמֹר

3:16 לֵךְ

4:7   וַיָּסִירוּ אֶת־רֹאשׁוֹ
so V.

7:1, 4; 10:1; 11:1,2:
  12:18; 13:1,23,30,36;
  15:1,7,32; 16:16;
  17:21; 19:26 (P v. 25)
      וַיְהִי

7:3   לֵךְ

11:1   וַיִּשְׁתַּחוּ

11:15 בַּסֵּפֶר לֵאמֹר

11:22 וַיָּבֹא

12:3   וַתִּגְדַּל

12:16 וַיָּבֹא

13:12 אַל־תְּעַנֵּהָ
       אֶת־הַנְּבָלָה הַזֹּאת

13:28 רְאוּ נָא

14:10 יֹסִיף

15:5   וְהֶחֱזִיק לוֹ

15:19 וְשׁוּב

15:27 הֲרוֹאֶה

16:13 הָלֹךְ

17:9   אָמַר

18:2   וַיְשַׁלַּח דָּוִד אֶת־הָעָם

18:21 וַיִּשְׁתַּחוּ כּוּשִׁי לְיוֹאָב

18:26 וַיִּרָא הַצֹּפֶה אִישׁ אַחֵר רָץ (וַיֹּאמֶר) הַמֶּלֶךְ גַּם־זֶה מְבַשֵּׂר

19:25 וְלֹא עָשָׂה רַגְלָיו

20:11 מִי אֲשֶׁר חָפֵץ בְּיוֹאָב

20:14 וַיִּקָּהֲלוּ

22:4   מְהֻלָּל

23:23 מִן־הַשְּׁלֹשִׁים נִכְבָּד וְאֶל־הַשְּׁלֹשָׁה לֹא־בָא

24:13 וַיַּגֶּד־לוֹ עַד

24:22 וְיַעַל

Besides these cases, there are 18 examples in which P omits MT, following LXX, which are dealt with in a subsequent chapter.

IV. Paraphrasing MT

When the question is asked, "Is a translation a
literal or a free rendering of the original?" one looks
for further evidence besides the examples of misreading
the original text or of adding to or omitting portions
of the original. Free translation is evident in the
numerous cases in which P goes its own way, over against
MT and any of the other versions.

For one thing: Hebrew idioms were paraphrased:

1:12 and 16:3   בְּיַת   P   حقر

10:10 בָּ֫רַ֫ךְ P ב   15:18 עַל־יְדֵי֫וֹ   P   ܠܠܘܢ

11:11   הַדָּבָר הַזֶּה   P   ܘܐ ܗ ܝ

13:23   לְשִׁנְתַיִם יָמִים   P   ܚܕܪ ܡܪܠ

13:32 עַל־פִּי   P   17:5 כִּי מַה־בַּפִּיו P   ܦܡ ܘܐ ܛܒ

13:33 אֶל־שִׁנֵּם...יָבֵל־בְּגֵי   P   ܘ ܣܡܚ ...

    19:8 (P v. 7) עַל־לֵב   P   ܠܒܗ

    19:20 (P v.19) לְבוֹשׁ־מִ֫...אֶל־לֵבִי P   ܐܘ....ܘܠ ܠܚܠܘ

15:6 and 17:6   כַּדָּבָר הַזֶּה   P   ܚ ܚ ܗ

15:10   לֵאמֹר   P   ܘܩܡܥ ܣ

15:12   הַלֹּכֶ֫ד וְ֫רַב   P   ܨܠ ܨܡ ܠܝܐ

15:13 and 20:2   אִ֫ישׁ   P   حقر

    19:15 (P v. 14), 44 (P v. 43), 20:4 אִ֫ישׁ P ܠܗ

    19:43 (P v. 42)   כָּל־אִ֫ישׁ   P ܠܗܝ ܘܗܠܚ ܘܚܠ

15:6   אֲדֹנִי   P   ܚܩܪ ܘܚܠܘܝ

    19:42 (P v. 41)   וַאֲדֹנָ֫י P ܘ ܠܚܝ

17:6 לֵאמֹר P ܗܣܒ   18:5 לֵאמֹר P ,

19:36 (P v. 35) twice   אִם   P ܗ

19:36 (P v. 35) Interr. הֲ   P ܗ

19:37 (P v. 36) לָמָּה P ܗ

The paraphrasing of MT by P is shown in the following
examples in which synonymous expressions were used,
instead of a literal translation of the original:

1:21   הָרֵי בַגִּלְבֹּעַ (וּשְׂדֵי תְרוּמֹת P ܘܛܪܒܙ, ܘܒܪܙܛ PES ܡܣܒܙܛܒܪ

LXX ἀγροὶ ἀπαρχῶν 'A ἀφαιρεμάτων

V agri primitiarum   T בְּאַמָּה אֲלַלַיָּא

The only other use of ܒ;ܐ in II Sam. is 1:23
where the normal parallel is מֵ רֶד

H.L. Ginsberg[1] has made the suggestion that MT
goes back to הַתְהֹומֹת שַׂרְ ע, from which it became
corrupted. He has found a parallel in the
Ugaritic material which would correct MT here to
"nor upswellings of the deep."

2:13 three times בְּרֵכַ P ܠܒܬܐ̈ which everywhere
in II Sam. stands for בְּנַי except once = עֹלָם
LXX ἐπὶ τὴν κρήνην V piscina T בְּרֵכְתָּא
In 4:12 בְּרֵכָ P|ܐܒܬ; LXX ἐπὶ τῆς κρήνης
'A,ϵ κολυμβήθρας V piscinam   T בְּרֵכְתָּא

2:23 הַחֹנִי P ܣܥ ܡܝ LXX ψόαν
'A ἐνοπλισμόν   V. in inquine
Cf. 20:10 where הַחֹנִי becomes   ܐܠܝܣ

LXX ψόαν V in latere   T.   אֵחֹרֵי רַ בְּמֶשׁ

In 3:27 הַמֶּשׁ is given correctly ܠܒܬ ܐܘ

3:35   וַיָּבֹא P. ܛܒܠ ܘ

LXX ἦλθεν V venisset T   וַיַּתָא

3:39 וַאָנֹכִי הַ רַךְ P. ܠ ܡܘ ܡܠܠ, ܘܐܢܐ

LXX συγγενὴς καὶ κατεσταμένος ·A, Σ ἁπαλὸς

V delicatus et unctus T   וְיַדִּים וְמָשֵׁ·

רַךְ means tender in years or delicately nurtured,

Gen. 33:13; Deut. 28:54. Neither meaning is

appropriate to David, who was certainly a mature

man and who had been brought up in hardship. It

is moreover difficult to connect the word with

what follows; "tender though anointed king" is

perhaps possible but how does it apply to the

situation? LXX[L] makes the clause apply to Abner

and translates συγγενὴς καὶ καθισταμένος ὑπὸ τοῦ

βασιλέως. The Jewish Version renders it well,

"And I am this day weak and just anointed king."

6:6 וַיִּשְׁמְטוּ· P. ܐܒܠ ܠܐܝ, LXX ὅτι περιέσπασεν αὐτὸν

V Quoniam calcitrabant boves et declinaverunt

eam   T   אֲרֵי בִ·רַקִּ·וּ ת·וֹרְ·תָ·ה

וַיִּשְׁמְטוּ· is a rare word and the passages in which

it occurs throw little light on its meaning here.

In II Kings 9:33 it is used transitively of throw-

ing a person out of a window. It would therefore

be natural to interpret it here as "the oxen cast
it down". But the object would almost certainly
be expressed, if this were the meaning. Another
meaning of the verb is "to release a debt" and
we might conjecture that the oxen "slipped",
losing their foothold. The LXX seems to find
the object expressed and so with T   בְּגֹרֶן
V calcitrabant seems to be a conjecture.

6:7 עַל־הַשַּׁל P   ܣܝ ܐܘ ܘ ‖LXX^B ⊐
LXX^A ἐπὶ προπετείᾳ 'A ἐπὶ τῇ ἐκνοίᾳ
V super temeritate   עַל דְּאַשְׁלֵי
There is no Hebrew word שַׁל known to us. The
other Vss. seem to go back to a common source
which interpreted the word by the Aramaic שְׁלִי
שְׁלָא "to err". It is quite likely that MT con-
stitutes the mutilated remains of the parallel
in I Chron. 13:10 עַל [אֲשֶׁר] שָׁלַח [יָדוֹ] עַל
6:16 עִיר P ܣ ܟܠܘܢ LXX πόλεως
V civitatem   T   לְקַרְתָּא
6:20 לְבָרֵךְ P ܠܝ ܘ ܒܪܟ LXX εὐλογῆσαι
V ut benediceret   T   לְבָרָכָא
8:1 מֶתֶג הָאַמָּה P ܦܓܘ ܐܠܒ
LXX ἀφωρισμένην 'A Τὸν Χαλινὸν τοῦ ὑδραγωγίου
V fraenum tributi T תְּקֹון אֲמָתָא
MT "the bridle of the cubit" is obscure. From

its being taken "from the hands of the
Philistines" we infer that it was some tangible
possession, probably a piece of property. The
parallel in I Chron. 18:1 אֶת גַּת וּבְנֹתֶיהָ
reads or interprets מֶתֶג as גַּת and supposing
"Gath the mother" to include her dependent
villages. The commentators have taken אַמָּה
to be an equivalent to אֵם as sometimes used in
Hebrew for a city (metropolis). Again מֶתֶג
could be taken to mean "power" or "suzerainty"
and it could mean that David assumed the power
or threw off the yoke. But it is difficult
to see why in such a prose account, such a
figurative expression as "the bridle of the
metropolis" should be used. P guessed that it
meant a definite place or piece of territory
and thus made a proper name of it.

8:4 וַיִּלְכֹּד P ܙܒܢ̄ o LXX προκατελάβετο
V captis   T אֲסַר

9:6 הֵנָּה P ܐܝܠܝܢ LXX ἴδου
V adsum   T נָּה

10:17 עָלָיו וַיִּלָּחֲמוּ P ܘ̄ܟ̄ܠܘ ܥܡ ... LXX ἐπολέμησαν μετ' αὐτοῦ
V pugnaverunt contra eum T וְאִתְכְּנָשׁוּ קְרָבָא עֲלֵיהּ

11:9 אֶת P ܥܡ LXX μετά

V cum   T עִם

11:15   וְיֻבּוֹ P ܬܒ ܘܣ·   LXX εἰσάγαγε

V ponite   T הָבוּ

MT וְיֻבּוֹ is here apparently used like יָבוֹ

But the original might well have been הָבֶאָ

as read by LXX.

11:24   הַמּוֹרִים P ܡܛܝ, ܣܒ   LXX οἱ τοξεύοντες

V sagittarii   T קַשָּׁתַיָּא

11:25   כָזֹה וְכָזֹה P ܬܝ ܚܙܡ ܬܗ

LXX φάγεται ἡ μάχαιρα   V consumit gladius

T חֲרַבָּא הֲדָא

11:25   וְהַחֲזֵק P ܘܣܩܡܣܘ

LXX κραταίωσον   V et exhortare eos

T וְהַחֲזֵק   LXX[L], some Mss. >

Perhaps P read it Qal, impv., in which case

it could be rendered as "prevail against her".

12:3   וַתְּהִי P ܬܟܣ | LXX ἦν

V eratque   T וַהֲוָת

12:9   אֶת־דְּבַר P ܡ ܩ ܗ ܡ   LXX λόγον

V verbum   T פִּתְגָמָא   Pfeiffer[2]

suggests that אֶת דְּבַר was inserted to avoid

blasphemy. LXX[L], θ read it אֶת יְהֹוָה

12:14   כִּי נִאֵץ נִאַצְתָּ אֶת־אֹיְבֵי יְהֹוָה

P ܙܐܘܙܟܚܠ ܠܚܠ ܚܚܒ, ܛܪ ܟ

LXX παροξύνων ..... ἐχθροὺς

'A διασύρων …. ἐχθροὺς

θ παροργίζων …. ἐναντίοις

V blasphemare fecisti inimicos Domini

T וְנָאֵץ נִאַצְתָּ אֶת־אֹיְבֵי לֹאֶן נִאַץ יהוה׃

C.D.Ginsburg[3] assumes the original text to
have been "thou hast greatly blasphemed
Jahweh" but that this was mitigated for fear
of disrespect by insertion of the word אֹיְבֵי
He quotes Rashi, "This is an alteration due
to the reverence for the glory of God".
Furthermore, he points out that נִאֵץ is Piel,
that it is found 13 times in that form but
never denotes Hiphil "to cause to blaspheme".
So as it stands, the text would mean "thou
hast greatly blasphemed the enemies of God",
which makes no sense. A similar insertion of
אֹיְבֵי took place, it seems to me, in I Sam.
25:22; LXX omits it, also.

12:31 וְהֶעֱבִיר אוֹתָם בַּמַּלְבֵּן P ܐܡ̈ܥܒܪ ܐܢܘܢ ܘ݂ܐܦܠ

LXX Καὶ ἔθηκεν ἐν τῷ πρίονι

V "traduxit in typo laterum" T וְיַעֲבֵר יָתְהוֹן׀

בְּשׁוּ·ק מַלְבְּ·נָ Driver[4] quotes Georg Hoffmann,
who in ZATW (1882) 53-72, made a study of the
word מַלְבֵּן, since Qere is taken to be the
correct form here. It denotes a brickmold;

thus by the simple emendation of וַיַּעֲבֵד
to הֶעֱבִיד David's supposed cruelty is mitigated to forced labor at making bricks. P by
using |ܐܢ ܥܒ "measure" hints at the correct
interpretation.

13:2 וַיִּפָּלֵא ... לַעֲשׂוֹת P ܗܘ ܩܫܐ ... ܘܐܡܪ

LXX ὑπέρογκον·· τοῦ ποῖησαιV difficile ..ageret

T לְמֶעְבַּד ... פַּלֵי

13:5 הַבִּרְיָה P ܠܚܡܐ LXX βρῶμα

V pulmentum T מַאֲכָלָא

13:37 וַיִּתְאַבֵּל P ܘܚܠܒ ... ܒܠܐ

LXX ἐπένθησεν V luxit T וְאִתְאַבַּל

By supposing that a scribe, who, having
accidently in the first instance passed over
vs.37b, discovered his mistake, inserted it
after 37a, and then repeated as much of 37a as
was necessary in order to render 38b intelligible and by emending by LXX[L], we might read
"And the spirit of the king longed to go out
to Absalom his son, for he was comforted for
the death of his son Amnon".

13:39 וַתְּכַל pL,Le,M ܘܐܬܬܠܝܬ pA ܘܗܘܐ

LXX ἐκόπασεν V cessavitque ...persequi

T וַתִּכְלֶה כָּלָה here means "to be consumed
with desire" as in Ps.84:3; 143:7. But here

it is feminine and could hardly have רוּחַ

as its subject. Therefore a feminine noun

is to be sought; LXX[L] evidently read וַתֵּכַל

רוּחַ הַמֶּלֶךְ and this is to be accepted; there-

fore; "and the spirit of the king longed".

14:6 וַיַּךְ P ܘܡܚܐ LXX ἔπαισεν

V percussit   T וּמְחָא

14:7 בְּנַפְשׁוֹ P ܒܩܪ̈ܐ ‖ LXX ἀντὶ τῆς ψυχῆς

14:11 גֹּאֵל הַדָּם P ܦܪܘܩ ‖ ‖ ܕܐܡܐ ‖

LXX ἀγχιστέα τοῦ αἵματος V proximi sanguinis

T גָּאֵל דְּמָא   גָּאֵל in the Pentateuch is

rendered by P as ܬܒܘܥ ܕܡܐ

14:14 נִדָּח P ܐܒܕ ‖ LXX ἐξεωσμένον

V abjectus est   T בְּדִירָא

14:19 אָם־אִישׁ P ܐܝܬ ܠܗ LXX ἔστιν

V est   T אִם אִית אָם is usually taken to

stand for יֵשׁ . However the form is unusual

and in the only other case of its occurrence,

Mic. 6:10, the text is dubious. It is possible

that it should be read אֱשׁוֹב , for which

therefore P ܐܝܬ ܠܗ may be cited.

14:20 סַבֹּב P ܠܡܚܕܪ ‖ LXX περιελθεῖν

V vertere   T לְאַסְחָרָא

14:21 עָשִׂיתִי זֹאת הַדָּבָר הַזֶּה

P ܠܗܕܐ ‖ ܠ ‖ ܠܡܚܕܪ ‖ so Mss.

LXX ἐποίησα   V feci   T עָֽשֶׂה

15:1 קִ֫אישׁ P ܓܒܪܐ܂ LXX ἄνδρας

V viros   T גַּבְרָ֨א

15:2 הַשַּׁ֫עַר דֶּ֫רֶךְ יַ֫ד עַל P ܥܠ ܝܕ܂ ܐܘܪܚܐ ܕܬܪܥܐ

LXX ἀνὰ χεῖρα τῆς ὁδοῦ τῆς πύλης

V juxta introitum portae

T עַל כְּבַש אוֹרַח תַּרְעָא T

15:4 וְשָׁ֫פְטִ֫יו P ܘܕܝܢܐ LXX καὶ κρίσις

LXX^L > V juste   T וְשָׁ֫פֵֽט׃

15:5 לוֹ וְהֶחֱזִ֫יק יָד֫וֹ אֶת־וְשָׁ֫לַ֫ח P ܩ ܪܡ ܗܘܐ ܡܝ

LXX ἐξέτεινεν ⋯ καὶ ἐπελαμβάνετο

V extendebat manum suam et apprehendens

T וּמוֹשִׁיט יָת יְדֵיהּ וּמַתְקִ֫יף בֵּֽיהּ T 30 Mss. בּוֹ

15:6 וַֽיְגַנֵּב P ܘܢܟܠܐ LXX ἰδιοποιεῖτο

V solicitabat   T וּגְנַ֫ב׃   This evidently
means "stole the understanding" or "deceived
the heart"; cf. Gen. 31:20, where Jacob deceived Laban.

15:13 הָֽיָה P ܘܗܘܐ LXX ἐγενήθη

V sequitur   T אַ֫תָּֽא׃

15:14 וּנְ֫ס־תִּ֫הְֽיֶ֫ה־לֹא P ܡܛܠ ܗ

LXX οὐκ ἔστιν V neque erit T וּנְ֫ס־תִּ֫הְֽיֶ֫ה לֹא

15:23 קוֹל P ܩܠܐ LXX φωνῇ V voce   T קָל

15:28 דָּבָ֫ר P ܡܠܐ LXX ῥῆμα V sermo   T פִּתְגָּֽמָא

15:32 וּלְקָרָאת֫וֹ P ܘܠܐ ܠ ܘܠܐ

LXX εἰς ἀπαντὴν αὐτῷ V occurrit ei

T וַיֵּלֶךְ לִקְרָאתֵיהּ‏

15:32   עַד־הָרֹאשׁ P ‏   LXX ἕως τοῦ Ῥωὶς 'A ἕως τῆς ἄκρας

Ε εἰς τὴν ἄκραν V summitatem montis

T עַד רֵישׁ טוּרָא‏

15:34   וַעֲנִי עַבְדָךְ P ‏   The Vss. follow MT. It is possible that

וַעֲנִי עַבְדָךְ was taken from the line above.
The Hebrew is awkward but the sense is apparently something like this: "thy servant will
I be, O king; thy father's servant was I
formerly and now I am thy servant."

16:1   מֵרֹאשׁ P ‏   LXX ἀπὸ τῆς Ῥωὶς 'A, Ε ἀπὸ τῆς ἄκρας

V montis verticen   T מֵרֵישׁ‏

16:1,2 קַיִץ P ‏   LXX φοίνικες

V palatharum   T דְּבֵלְתָּא   קַיִץ‏
is rendered elsewhere in OT as ‏ (in Gen.
8:22; Am.3:15; Zech. 14:8; Jer. 40:10,12;
Ps.74:17; and Prov. 30:25). Or as ‏ in
Is. 16:9 and Jer. 48:32. Also as ‏ in Am.
8:1,2.

16:2   לָמוֹ P ‏ / ‏ LXX τί V quid T לָמָה‏

16:2   לַחֲמֹרִים P ‏

LXX ἐπικαθῆσθαι   V ut sederant   T וַיֵּשְׁבוּ

16:4   וְיִשְׁתַּחוּ   P ܘܣܓܕ

LXX προσκυνήσας   V oro   T מִשְׁתַּחֲוֶה

16:19   בְנוֹ אֶפְעַל   P ܒܪ ܐܦܠ

LXX ἐνώπιον τοῦ υἱοῦ αὐτοῦ

V filio regis   T לִפְנֵי בְנוֹ כֵּן

16:21   אֶת־אֲבִי אָבִיךָ אֲשֶׁר   P ܘܐܪܡܝ ܦܠܚܬܐ ܘܐܬܚܫܒ

LXX Κατήσχυνας   V foederavis   T אֶת־אָבִיךָ

The combination found in MT here is found

nowhere else. It is possible that the Hiphil

was originally written.

17:2   עָלָיו וְיָבֹא   P ܘܐܬܐ ܥܠܘܗܝ   LXX επελεύσομαι

V irruens   T וְיָבֹא עָלָיו

17:3   מְבַקֵּשׁ   P ܒܥܐ ܐܢܬ   LXX σὺ ζητεῖς

V quaeris   T בַּקֵּשׁ

17:15   זִקְנֵי   P ܘܠܩܫܝ   LXX τοῖς πρεσβυτέροις

V senioribus   T זִקְנֵי

17:16   פֶּן־יְבֻלַּע לַמֶּלֶךְ וּלְכָל־הָעָם אֲשֶׁר

P ܘܕܠܡܐ ܢܒܠܥ ܡܠܟܐ ܘܟܠܗ ܥܡܐ

LXX μή ποτε καταπείσῃ τὸν βασιλέα

καὶ πάντα τὸν λαὸν τὸν μετ' αὐτοῦ

V ne forte absorbeatur rex et omnis populus

qui cum eo est.

וְדֵלְמָא יִתְבְּלַע מַלְכָּא וְכָל־עַמָּא דִּי עִמֵּהּ

Literally, MT means "lest it be swallowed up

to the king"; thus, "lest the king be swallowed
up". It is figurative language for "be undone"
or "be destroyed", which P represents.

17:19 ‏נֹורְדִיפֹו‎ P ܡܘ; LXX ἀραφωθ

V ptisanas   T ‏הַקְּיֹצ‎ The meaning is uncertain.
No root ‏רוד‎ or ‏דיר‎ with a suitable meaning is
known. LXX merely transliterates MT; V follows
'A, Ɛ who have πτισάνες LXX[L], θ have παλάθας
P means "hulled" (or "crushed) barley", which
probably comes from 'A, Ɛ.

17:19 ‏דָּבָר וְנֹודַע וְלֹא‎ P ܘܠܐ ܝܪܥ ܡܕܡ

LXX Καὶ οὐκ ἐγνώθη ῥῆμα V sic latuit res
T ‏וְלֹא אִתְיִדַע פִּתְגָמָא‎

17:20 ‏בְּמֹ־טָב‎ P ‏ܘܛܥܡ ܠܗܘܢ‎, LXX μικρόν

V transierunt festinanter gustata paululum
aqua   T ‏בְּבַר עֲבְרוּ יַרְדְנָא‎ This is
hapax legomenon in OT. It is doubtful whether
any satisfactory meaning to this can be found.
The so-called Arabic and Assyrian parallels
offer no solution, nor do the Versions.
Driver[5] comes to the conclusion: "If the word
be not corrupt, it is one of which the meaning
is unknown."

18:4 ‏אֶעֱשֶׂׄוּן‎ P ‏ܐܥܒܕ‎, LXX ποιήσω

V faciam   T ‏אֶעֱבֵיד‎

18:5 לְאַט־לִי P ܐܬܒܛܠܘ ܠܝ LXX φείσασθέ μου
V servate mihi   T אֲטַעֲנוּ לִי

18:8 נָפֹצֶית P ܡܒܕܪ LXX διεσπαρμένος
V dispersum   T מְבַדְּרִין

18:8 אָכַל הַ P ܐܘܟܠ LXX κατέφαγεν
V voraverat   T מְקַטֵּל

18:12 עַל־כַּפַּי P ܥܠ ܐܝܕܝ LXX ἵστημι ἐπὶ τὰς χειράς μου
V appenderes in manibus meis   T עַל כַּף יְדָי

18:18 אֵין־לִי בֵן P ܠܝܬ ܠܝ LXX υἱὸς V filium   T לֵית לִי בַר

18:18 יָד אַבְשָׁלוֹם P ܩܝܡܬܐ LXX ἀναμνῆσαι
V monimentum   T אַתְרָא

19:1 מִי יִתֵּן P (18:33) ܡܢ LXX δώη
V tribuat   T לְוָי

19:25 כָבֵּס P (vs.24) ܐܫܝܓ LXX ἀπέπλυνεν
V laverat   T חַוַּר

19:28 וַיְרַגֵּל בְּעַבְדְּךָ P (vs.27) ܘܐܟܠ ܩܪܨܝ LXX μεθώδευσεν ὁ δοῦλός σου
V accusavit me servum tuum   T וְאַסְטַן עַל עַבְדָּךְ

19:29 וּמַה־יֶּשׁ־לִי עוֹד P (vs.28) ܠܡܢܐ ܠܝ LXX καὶ τί ἐστίν μοι ἔτι V aut quid possum ultra

19:30 לָמָּה P (vs.29) ܠܡܢ LXX ἵνα τί V quid T לְמָא

19:32 אֶת־הַיַּרְדֵּן P (vs.31) ܝܘܪܕܢܢ LXX τὸν Ἰορδάνην V fluvium T יַת יַרְדְּנָא

20:3 וַיִּתְּנֵ֔ם) P ܐܣܠܡ LXX ἔδωκεν

V tradidit T וַיִּתְּנֵ֔ם·ן

20:6 אֶל־אֲבִישַׁ֣י P ܝܘܐܒ / ܠ LXXB Ἀβεισά

LXXA Ἀβισαει V Abisai T אֲבִישַׁ֣י

P may be due to inner Syriac error by
metathesis for MT. Or P may have been influenced by the mention of Joab in the following verses. Since Joab was in disgrace
at this time, it was more natural that Abishai
be called upon. Joab probably accompanied
the expedition in a subordinate position
but his energy and habit of command made
him the real leader.

20:6,7,10,13 רְדֹף֙ ן P ܪܗܛ o LXX καταδίωξον

V persequere T רְדֹף֙·ן

20:8 מַדּ֣וֹ P ܥܛܦ)) LXX μανδύαν

V tunica T ≻. This should be read מַדּ֣וֹ
as in I Sam. 17:38,39.

20:8 וְהֻא־יָצָ֣א וְיִפֹּֽל) P ܘܗܘ ܢܦܩ ܥܠ ܘܩܛܠ
LXX καὶ αὐτὴ ἐξῆλθεν καὶ ἔπεσεν

V motu egredi poterat et percutere

וַיִּפֹּֽל יָצָ֣א וְהֻא MT is involved and obsure.
If the sword fell, the author should tell us
that Joab picked it up again before reaching
Amasa. P gives us a clue by stating that

"his sword rested on his hips like a dagger";
then it would be easy for Joab to reach or, as
P also states, "his hand fell upon his sword".
This is a good rendering but P alone is not
sufficient evidence to establish it.

20:9 וַיִּקֶן P ܢܚܘܬ o LXX ἐκράτησεν
V tenuit T וַיֹּחֶז

20:10 יִשְׁפֹּךְ P ܘܐܫܕ o LXX ἐξεχύθη
V effudit T יִשְׁפֹּ

20:12 בְּתוֹךְ P ܒܓܘ o LXX ἐν μέσῳ
V in media T בַּגַּיְ

20:12 הַבָּא P ܐܬܐ ₁ LXX ἐρχόμενον
V transeuntes T הָבָּאִי

20:15 בְּאָבֵל P ܒܐ‌ܒ‌ܠ LXX προτειχίσματι
V obsessa est urba T בַּסֹּלְלָה וַיִּשְׁפְּכוּ

20:18 שָׁאֹל P ܫ‌ܐ‌ܠ‌ܘ The versions follow MT.
P exegeted, for the previous verb is שָׁאֹל
thus the idea of "inquiring of the prophets"
came to mind instead of "inquiring in Abel".

20:18 הֵתַמּוּ P ܛ‌ܒ‌ܣ‌ܪ LXX ἐξέλιπον
V perficiebant T אַשׁ‌ַמּוּ הֵם
Possibly P misread MT as הֵתַמּוּ

20:19 אֱמוּנֵי P ܐ‌ܡ‌ܢ‌ܗ LXX τῶν στηριγμάτων
V veritatem T בַּצֹּרִי הַ‌ת
20:21 יָדוֹ P ܐ‌ܝ‌ܕ‌ܗ LXX τὴν χεῖρα αὐτοῦ

V manum   T   יָדִי

21:15   וַיָּעַף   דָּוִד   P (vs.16)   ܘܪܡ , ܐܬܡܠܝ ,ܣ

LXX ἐπορεύθη   V deficiente T   וְאִשְׁתַּנִּיו׃

MT is suspicious and probably corrupt. If the
Philistines had attacked David when weary, a
more explicit statement would have been made.
A notice of the place where the contest
occurred is here required and it might well be
that by emendation וְיֵשֶׁב׃ בְּגֹב could be the
correct reading. Then וַיָּעַף דָּוִד might well
be concealing the name of the Philistine and
perhaps a verb as well, of which וַיֹּאמֶר of 16b
would be the sequel.

21:22 וַיִּפְּלוּ׃ P   ܐܬܒܠܥܘ LXX ἔπεσαν

V ceciderunt   T   וְאִתְקְטֵלוּ׃

23:4 דֶּשֶׁא׃ P ܥܡܪܐ , LXX χλόης V herba

23:5   כִּי־כָל־יִשְׁעִי וְכָל־חֵפֶץ

P   ܟܠܗ ܝܫܘܥܝ , ܘܟܠܗ ܨܒܝܢܝ

LXX ὅτι πᾶσα σωτηρία μου καὶ πᾶν θέλημα
V cuncta enim salus mea et omnis voluntas

T   אֲרֵי כָל צָבִי וְכָל צוֹרְכִי׃   T

P reversed the order and by metathesis and
inner Syriac error arrived at   ܨܒܝܢܝ

for   ܝܫܘܥܝ

23:5 יַצְמִיחַ׃ P ܐܦܠܚ LXX οὐ μὴ βλαστήσῃ

V germinet   T תַצְמִיחַ   יַצְמִיחַ

is unintelligible and perhaps   יַצְלִיחַ

"cause it to prosper" would be a good emenda-

tion.

23:6   מֻנָד P ܡܣܠܝ LXX ἐρωσμένη V evellentur

מֻנָד does not seem appropriate; it is either

the passive of נָדַד (Job 18:18; 20:8) or of

הֵנִיד (Ps. 36:12).   In the former case it

would mean "to chase away"; in the latter,

"to put to flight".   But the word excites

suspicion; for it is not one that would

naturally be applied to thorns.

23:7   יִמָּלֵא P ܢܬܡܠܐ LXX πλήρης

V armabitur   וְהַבַרְזֶל לִי וְעֵץ

יִמָּלֵא on the analogy of II Kings 9:24, means

literally "fills himself", i.e. insofar as the

hand using the weapon is concerned.   LXX[L]

ἐὰν μή points to אִם־לֹא but the negative does

not fit.

23:11   לַחַיָּה P ܠܚܝܘܬܐ LXX πλήρης

V plenus   T חַיָּא

23:15   בְּשַׁעַר P ܣܩ ܬܪܥܐ LXX ἐν τῇ πύλῃ

V portam   T בִּתְרַע

23:16   בְּשַׁעַר P ܣܩ ܬܪܥܐ LXX ἐν τῇ πύλῃ

V portam   T בִּתְרַע

23:18 twice; 19; 22. שֹׁלֵשֹׁים P ܐܝܠ LXX τρισίν

V tris   התֹשֵֹׁלֹ The sense requires that

we read שֹׁלֵשׁים here with 2 Mss. and P.

23:19 צֵאֵת לֹא הֹשֹׁלֹשֵׁים עֵד וּ P/ܩ ܢܚ ܐܝܠ ܐܠ ܦܡܪܘ

LXX, 'A, Σ ἕως τῶν τριῶν οὐκ ἦλθε

V ad tres primos non pervenerat

T   אֹטֹא אֹל וֹרֹד גֹ נֹתֹתֹצֹ)

23:23 וֹתֹשֹׁמֹעֹתֹ P ܠܛܠܠ ܐܡܚܡ ܠܛܒ܂

LXX εἰς τὰς ἀκοὰς αὐτοῦ

V auricularium, a secreto T תֹּאֹעֹטֹשֵׁא

23:34 בֹצֹמֹעֹה בֶּן־הֹ P ܡܕ ܛܒܠ ܘ

LXX υἱὸς τοῦ Μαχαχααχεί   V filii

T הֹבֹצֹתֹ בֶּן־הֹ is the gentile adjective

of מֹעֹכֹה; perhaps, however, הֹמֹעֹכֹתֹ בֹּתֹ

should be read.

24:1 צֹרֹוֹ תֹיֹהֹ P ܠܒܠ ܙܘ LXX ἐκκαῆναι

θ θυμωθῆναι V irasci   T צֹפֹ תֹמֹ

24:2 הֹאֹלֹ בֹּ P ܝ ܘ܂ LXX ὁ βασιλεύς V rex T אֹפֹצֹ

24:2 וֹדֹעֹת P ܐܠ ܘ also adds ܐܡܚ ܡܚܐܘ܂

LXX γνώσομαι V sciam   T אֹעֹד)

24:7 וֹתֹעֹ וֹדֹהֹ יֹ הֹ גֹּ־עֹרֹיֹ רֹיֹר־מֹבֹצֹרֹי וֹבֹאֹוֹ

שֹׁבֹעֹ בֹּאֹר הֹוֹדֹהֹ נֹגֹ־אֹל וֹיֹאֹוֹ וֹדֹנֹ תֹקֹפֹ וֹהֹ

P ܠܡܚܚܒܘ܂ ܙܗ ܒܠܘ܂ ܠܘܦ ܛܒ ܡܪ ܘܠܘ܂

ܘܠܘ ܐܙ ܡܠܚ ܡܗܘ ܂ ܡܠܚܚ ܡܡܚ ܒ܂ ܡܗܘ ܡܐܡܘ܂

ܠܪܝ ܗܙܚ ܠܘ ܡܚܐ ܠܪ ܡܒ ܡ ܟܛܒܠ ܚ ܐܝܠܐ ܂ ܠܘ ܪܝܣܘ ܗܡܘ

For the most part, the other versions follow
MT.

24:9   וַיְתֵּן P ܘܝܗܒ LXX ἔδωκεν V dedit T וִיהַב

24:10 וַיַּךְ P ܕܚ , ܡܚܐ LXX σφόδρα
        V valde   T לַחֲדָא

24:10   הַעֲבֶר־נָא אֶת־עֲוֹן עַבְדֶּךָ
        P   ܘܥܒܪ ܠܗ ܚܕܐ ܛܒܐ
        LXX παράβιβασον τὴν ἀνομίαν
        V ut transferas iniquitatem servi tui
              אַעְבַּר כְּעַן יַת חוֹבָא דְעַבְדָּךְ

24:12 נֹשֵׂא P ܐܛܠ LXX αἴρω V datur   T רָמֵי
        LXX gives the meaning well: "lift up" or "hold".
        The root נָשַׂא is rare (Is.40:15; Lam. 3:28);
        perhaps the parallel in I Chron. 21:10 נֹטֶה
        is more probable.

24:13 תָּנֻס P ܬܥܪܘܩ LXX φεύγειν
        V fugies   T הֲתֶהֱוֵי עֲרִיק

24:15 עַד עֵת מוֹעֵד P ܠܥܠܡ ܬܫܠܡ
        LXX ἕως ὥρας ἀρίστου V ad tempus constitutum
        T מֵעִדָּן דְּמִתְנְכִיס תְּמִירָא וְעַד דְּמִתְעֲבַד
        The meaning is altogether uncertain. "To the
        appointed time" cannot be right, for it appears
        from vs. 16 that the plague was stopped before
        the three days had terminated. T paraphrased:
        "from the time when the daily burnt offering

was killed until it was offered", and so Rashi
and Kimchi; another explanation, cited by
Kimchi, is "until midday" (cf. LXX ἕως ὥρας
ἀρίστου P ܡܬܠ ܠܗ   )

24:16 אֶל־הָרָעָה יהוה וַיִּנָּחֶם P |ܠ ܐܒ ܟܠܒ ܡ
      LXX, 'A, Σ παρακλήθη   Θ μετεμελήθη
      V misertus est .... super afflictione
      T   אַשְׁיָתָא לָהּ ... דַּיּ)

24:17 הֶעֱוֵיתִי P ܠܢ ܠ ܐ   LXXB >
      LXXᴬ ἡμάρτηκα V inique egi T הֶחֱוֵ֥יתִי

24:20 וַיַּשְׁקֵף P ܣܐܠ ܐ LXX διέκυψεν
      V conspiciensque   T וְאִסְתְּכַל

24:20 וַיֵּצֵא P ܢܦܩ ܐ LXX ἐφῆλθεν
      V egressus   T   וּנְפַק)

24:24 כֶּסֶף שְׁקָלִים P ܪ ܙ ܠܐܠ
      LXX ἐν ἀργυρίῳ σίκλων V argenti siclis
      T   בְּכֶסֶף סַלְעִין

24:25 וַיֵּעָתֵר P ܐܠ ܐܠ LXX ἐπήκουσεν
      V propitiatus est   T קַבֵּיל

V. Proper Names

In the LXX, Swete found that Hebrew proper names
were transliterated in indeclinable forms for the most
part, although some well-known names received Greek
terminations and were declined.[6] Driver points out
that the Mss. of the Septuagint translators must have
been written in an early form of the square character,
perhaps a transitional Palestinian alphabet, in which
ן and ’ , ד and ר , ב and כ , ב and ם , ה,ח and final
ם resembled each other very closely.[7] This must also
have been true of the Mss. used by the translators of
the Peshitto, as will be noted below.

Just as in the LXX, when the MT was not understood,
P made proper names into common nouns and vice versa.
In a few cases, P corrected the MT. In others, the
LXX influenced P over against MT. There are still
other instances which cannot be placed in any of these
categories and must be dealt with individually.

1. Proper names are regarded as common nouns:

5:18, 22; 23:13   בְּעֵ֫מֶק רְפָאִ֖ים

P. 5:18, 22   ܥܘܡܩܐ ܘܢܓܪ̈ܐ

P 23:13   ܥܘܡܩܐ ܘܢܓܪ̈ܐ   so T.

In this case P was influenced by LXX which
has Κοιλάδα τῶν Τιτάνων in 5:18 and 22 but
Κοιλάδα τῶν Ραφαειμ in 23:13. On the other

hand, V has in valle Raphaim in 5:18, 22 but
in valle gigantum in 23:13.[8]

6:2   מִבַּעֲלֵי יְהוּדָה P أ‍ﺴﻮ ‚ ﺍﻩ

following LXX ἀπὸ τῶν ἀρχόντων

[Ἀ,Σ ἐχόντων] Ἰούδα

V de viris Juda. In I Chron.
13:6 it appears as   בְּבַעֲלָה אֶל קִרְיַת

יְעָרִים אֲשֶׁר לִיהוּדָה' In Josh. 15:60; 18:14,
Qiryath Ye'arim is called   קִרְיַת־בַּעַל
Therefore יְהוּדָה בַּעֲלֵ must be restored here.
At first it was changed to בַּעֲלֵי יְהוּדָה
by dittography. Then מ was prefixed to
connect it with the preceding clause.

6:6   נָכוֹן P ܦܒܶܢ supported by 'A ἑτοίμης
who often translates proper names into common
nouns. T also makes it a common adjective
מְתַקֵּן. MT is supported by LXX[A] Ναχών
and V Nachon. In the parallel (I Chron. 13:9)
it appears as כִּידֹן and LXX[A] Χειλω.[9]

8:18   וְהַפְּלֵתִי P ܦܠܬ with T. פְלַיְתִי
but MT is supported by LXX[B] ὁ φελεττεί
and LXX[A] ℛφελεθθει   and V Phelethi.

15:17   בֵּית הַמֶּרְחָק P ܟܝ ܡܚܩ following
LXX μακραν. V has procul a domo and
T נֶאֱזַב רָחִיק פֹּין. The Revised Version margin

has "the Far House", probably the last house
in Jerusalem in the direction of the Mount of
Olives.

17:17   בְּעֵין - רֹגֵל P ‏ܡܢ‎, ‏ܐܣܬ‎ following T בְּעֵין
קָצֵ֖ינ but LXX ἐν τῇ πηγῇ 'Ρωγήλ
and V fontem Rogel. In Josh. 15:7 and 18:16
P ‏ܐܝܢ‎,, ‏ܡܝܢ‎ an example of inner Syriac corruption
, for ‏j‎ . Here T also עֵין קָצֵ֖ינ

21:6   בְּגִבְעַת P ‏ܒܓܒܥ‎ ‏ܗ‎ following T
בְּגִבְעָת֖א but LXX, 'A, Ɛ ἐν Γαβαών
and V Gabaa. Cf. 23:29 MT מִגִּבְעַת
P ‏ܡܢ‎ ‏ܓܒܥ‎ ‏jܬܐ‎ also with T מִגִּבְעָת֖א but
LXX Γαβαὲθ while V de Gabaath.

21:19   אֶת־גָּלְיָת֙ הַ֙ P ‏ܠܘܬ‎, ‏ܡܢ‎
By comparison with the parallel in I Chron.
20:5 it can be seen that אֶת־גָּלְיָת found its way
into the text by error from the line below,
although the error must be older than LXX[BA]
'Αρωργείμ. Driver notes that 20 other LXX mss.
have Αρωρι [10]   יָעְר֖י should, with I Chron.
20:5 Qere, LXX, and P be read.

23:8   יֹשֵׁב֩ בַּשֶּׁ֨בֶת תַּחְכְּמֹנִ֜י
P   ‏ܠܒ‎ ‏ܚܟܐܒܬ‎ ‏ܡܘܬܒ‎ ‏ܚܪܙ‎ ‏jܗ‎
MT is supported by LXX 'Ιεβόσθε ὁ Χαναναῖος
The passages in Chron. have: I Chr. 11:11

יִשׁבְעָם בֶּן חכמוני, and I Chr. 27:2   יָשָׁבְעָם

בֶּן זַבְדִּיאֵל .   יֹשֵׁב בַּשֶּׁבֶת

goes back to יֹשֵׁב בָּעֵל . Then בַּשֶּׁבֶת was sub-

stituted for בָּעֵל . The resultant יֹשֵׁב בַּשֶּׁבֶת

was corrupted to יֹשֵׁ ב בַּ שֶׁ בֶ ת   T.has

אֲנָא דְיָתֵב עַל כֻּרְסֵי דִינָא and V sedens in

cathedra and ⟩   תַּחְכְּמֹנִי.

23:11 הָרָרִי P ܛܘܪܪܐ ; ܘ ܛ following T טוּרָרָא.
MT is supported by LXX Ἀρουχαῖος   and V
Arari[11] Cf. 23:33 where MT הַהֲרָרִי also T
טוּרָרָא ויתיר.but P ܐܪܘ , ; ܘ ܛ LXX here
Ἀρωδείτης and V Orori.

23:25 הַחֲרֹדִי P ܛܘܪܪܐ ; ܘ ܛ as in vs. 11.Quite
likely P read הָרָרִי here as well. But T קֵן
חָרוֹד   LXX[B] Ῥουδαῖος and LXX[A] Ἀρουδαῖος
V de Harodi[12]

23:28 הָאֲחֹחִי P ܟܠܐ ; ܘ ܛ , MT is supported by
LXX[B] Ἀωείτης but LXX[A] Ἐλωείτης
T אֲחֹחִי and V Ahohites. It is possible that
P read הָרָרִי here and translated it as in v. 11,
25, and 33 but added ܘܐܚܘ .

   2. Common nouns are translated as proper names:
5:7,9,17; 23:14 הַמְּצֻדָה P ܠܘ ; ܛ MT is supported
by LXX περιοχήν and Ἀ'οχύρωμα. In II Sam.22:2
MT מְצֻדָתִי P ܐܠܡ.The parallel in Ps.18:3 so

also but LXX^{Sam.} ὀχύρωμα μοι   while LXX^{Ps.}

ἰσχύς μοι. In I Sam. 22:4,5; 24:23 is trans-

lated by P. as ܛܘܪܐ but in I Sam.23:14,19;

and 24:1,2 as ܒܝܬ ܨܝܕ . LXX is Μεσσαρά in

I. Sam 23:19 and 24:23, confusing ܕ and ܪ ; it

is ἐν Μασερὲμ in I Sam. 23:14; and ἐν τοῖς

στενοῖς   in I Sam. 24:1. I Sam.22:4,5

have περιοχῇ.

5:23,24   בְּבָאִים   pA,M,ES   ܒܟܐ

pL,Le,BH   ܟܕ ܒܟܐ   LXX Κλαυθμῶνος

reading בִּבְכָם, while 'A has τῶν ἀπίων

6:3   בַּגִּבְעָה?   P ܒܓܒܥܐ   LXX supports MT with

βουνῷ V in Gabaa   T בְּגִבְעָתָא.

24:5   וְאֶל־יַעְזֵר   P ܘܡܢ ܝܥܙܝܪ, o , following LXX^B

Ἐλιέζερ and LXX^A Ἐλιάζηρ.[13]

3. P follows LXX against MT

3:13; 6:16,20,21,23   מִיכַל   P ܡܠܟܘܠ with LXX

Μελχὸλ.

8:3,5,7,8,9,10,12   הֲדַדְעֶזֶר   P ܗܕܪ ܥܙܪ with

many Mss. and LXX Ἀδρααζηρ and V. T support:

MT.

20:24   אֲדֹרָם   P ܐܕܘܪܝܡ, with LXX Ἀδωνειράμ

but V Aduram and T אֲדוֹרָם. This word also

occurs in I Kings 12:18 where P also has

ܐܕܘܪܝܡ, but LXX^B Ἀραμ but LXX^A Ἀδωνιράμ.

V and T support MT.

21:18 בְּגוֹב P ܒܓܘܒ with LXX ἐν Γέθ, but V in Gob
and T בְּגוֹב.[14] The parallel in I Chron. 20:4
has בְּגֹוּר.

4. P emends MT

1:1 הָעֲמָלֵקִי P ܥܡܠܩܝܐ. According to usage elsewhere it should be הָעֲמָלֵקִי with 5 mss.

2:9 הַגְּשׁוּרִי P ܘܓܫܘܪܝ supported by V
Gessuri, perhaps correctly.[15] LXX[B] θασειρι
and LXX[A] θασουρ [16] T has אֲשֵׁר עַל וְכָל הַבֵּיתִ.

8:8 וּמִבְּטָח P ܛܒܚܬ ܡܢ, reading שֶׁבַח with
I Chron. 18:8 טִבְחַת (cf. Gen. 22:24).
LXX[B] Μασβακ and LXX[A] Μασβαχ.[17] V,T support MT.

8:17 וּשְׂרָיָה בֶּן אֲחִיטוּב P ܘܫܪܝܐ ܚܙ ܐܘܫܝܡ
MT is supported by LXX, V,T But most critics
accept this emendation by P.

20:25 MT[K] שְׁיָא MT[Q] שְׁוָא P ܣ̣ܪܝܐ. In 8:17 שְׂרָיָה
is the name of David's secretary, so P follows
that.

21:8 מִיכַל P ܪܒ, which stands everywhere in
P for רַב. MT is supported by LXX[B] Μιχολ
and LXX[A] Μελχολ but P is supported by LXX[L]
Μεροβ and T רַב, besides 2 Mss.

5. Confusion of Hebrew letters causes these cases:
8:12,13 בַּאֲרָם P ܒܐܕܘܡ, ܐܕܘܡ confusing ר and ד.

9 Mss., I Chron. 18:11 מֵֽאֲדֹ֔ם and LXX ἐκ τῆς Ἰδουμαίας.

15:8 בַּֽאֲרָ֖ם P ܒܐܕܘܡ, the same confusion of ד and ר.

20:1,2,6,7,10,13,21,22. שֶׁ֣בַע P ܣܒܥ, confusing ב and ע. MT is supported by LXX[BA] Σάβεε. V, T also.

20:26 הַיָּֽאִרִי P ܝܥܝܪ ܕ, confusing N and ע. MT is supported by LXX ὁ Ἰαρείν but LXX[L] ὁ Ἰεθέρ.

23:13 עֲדֻלָּ֖ם P ܓܪܠܐ, confusing ד and ר, as elsewhere (cf. Josh. 12:15; 15:35; I Sam. 22:1) But Mic. 1:15 ܥܕܠܡ and Neh. 11:30 ܐܕܘܠܡ. MT is supported by LXX Ὀδολλάμ [18] so V, T.

23:31 אֲבִֽי־עַלְבֹ֑ון P[L,Le,A,M] ܐܒܝܛܠܒܘܢ - P[BH] ܐܒܝܚܠܐ / - confusing ב and ע. MT is supported by LXX[A] Ἀειέλβων but the parallel in I Chron. 11:32 אֲבִיאֵ֔ל is supported by LXX[B] Ἀβιήλ and LXX[L] Ἀβιής. [19] V Abialbon T אֲבִיעַלְבֹ֑ון

23:32 יָשֵׁ֖ן P ܝܫܢ, confusing י and ו, ד and ר. The parallel in I Chron 11:34 is הָשֵׁ֖ם P ܚܫܘ. MT is supported by LXX Ἀσάν V Jassen and T יָשֵׁ֖ן [20]

23:33 הָאֲרָרִ֔י P ܐܪܪܝ, confusing ד and ר. MT is supported by LXX[A] Ἀραρείτης but

LXX[B] Ἑαραουρείτης   V de Orori

T   דְמַטּוּר גָבוֹת.

6.   P interprets MT

2:29   הַחֲבָרוֹן P ;ܐܶܝ ﺗﱡ Ḥ. MT is supported by
'A βεθωρῶν , while LXX Παρατείνουσαν.
V Beth-horon and T   בֵּתְחָרוֹן [21]. This is
hapax legomenon in the OT. Arnold[22] thinks
it represents an adverbial accusative of time
"All the half (sc. of the day)".

3:16; 16:5; 17:18 (cf. I Kings 2:8) MT   בַּחֻרִים
P ܝܶ ;ܐܢ ܐܠܐ P divided it thus: בְ[for
חֻרִים בֵּ[רִ. MT is supported by LXX[A]
βαουρειμ .[23] LXX[B] βαρακεί in 3:16; βαορείμ
in 17:18; βουρείμ in 16:5; βααθουρείμ in
I K. 2:8, followed by P. V follows MT.

T   צָפֵת

10:6   בֵּית רְחוֹב P ܪܘܡ ; בְ. MT is supported
by P of Jud. 18:28 ܪܘܡ ; ܐܠܐ (cf. P in
Num. 13:22 (MT vs. 21). V Rohob T בֵּ רְחוֹב תָ
LXX καί Ῥοώβ [24]

10:6,8 צוֹבָה אֲרָם P ܒܢܙ ܐܪܡ LXX[A] Συρίαν Σουβὰ
while LXX[B] > in 10:6 and Συρίας Σουβὰ
in 10:8 V, T follow MT.

21:19 בְּגֹב P > but adds ܠܠ ܣܡ Ḥ. MT is supported
by LXX[A]ἐν Γόβ , but LXX[B]ἐν Ῥόμ.V, T follow MT.

23:8 　Syriac text　 עֶזְנִ֛י בְּדִ֖ינֹ הוּא P Syriac

The parallel in I Chron. 11:11 reads עוֹרְרָ הוּא

אֶת־חֲנִי֖תֹו while P Syriac

Syriac ... It is probable that P of Sam.

interpreted MT to mean something resembling

the parallel in Chron. but where P in both

Sam. and Chron. got 　Syriac　 it

is impossible to explain. Driver[25] states

that most modern critics read עוֹרֵר אֶת־

חֲנִ֖יתֹו with the parallel in Chron.

LXX 'Ἀδεινὼν ὁ 'Ἀσωναῖος

23:38 יִתְרִ֖י P Syriac , LXX[B] 'Εθθεναῖος

LXX[A] Τεθριτης V Jethrites T יִתְרֹ דִּמְן

24:7 הַחִוִּ֖י P Syriac MT is supported by LXX

Τοῦ Εὐαίου V Hevaei and T חִוָאֵי

7. Metathesis explains:

17:27 וְשֹׁבִ֖י P Syriac / MT is supported by

LXX 'Οὐεσβεί. This is hapax legomenon in

OT. V Sobi and T וְשׁוֹבִי

23:31 הַבַּרְחֻמִ֖י P Syriac. The parallel in

I Chron. 11:33 is הַבַּחֲרוּמִ֖י. Driver[26]

thinks it should be הַבַּחֻרִמִ֖י, cf. 3:16.

MT is supported by LXX[A] βαρωμειτης but

LXX[B] βαρδιαμειτης. V de Beromi and

T דְּמִבַּחֻרִים .

8. Miscellaneous

1:1 צִקְלַג P ܨܥܠܘܢ here as elsewhere in OT (Josh.
15:31; 19:5; I Sam. 27:6; 30:1, 14,26; II Sam.
4:10; I Chron. 4:30; 12:1,21; Neh. 11:28) MT
is supported by LXX Σεκελὰγ .[27] The presence
of the ו in P may be due to dissimilation.
V and T follow MT.

2:8,10,12,15; 3:8,14,15; 4:5,8,8,12. MT אִישׁ־בֹּשֶׁת
P ܐܫܒܫܘܠ. If we assume בֹּשֶׁת was substituted
for בַּעַל, then אִישׁ־בַּעַל must have been the
original reading. Cod. 93, Holmes, 'A, Σ, θ
read εἰσβαὰλ. I Chron. 8:33; 9:39 have
אִישׁבַּעַל but P here also ܐܫܒܫܘܠ.
It is possible that ܐܫܒܫܘܠ is a corruption of ܐܫܒܥܠ and ܐܫܒܥܠ

5:15 יִבְחָר P;ܥܘܒܪ LXX[B] Ἐβεὰρ LXX[A] Ἰεβὰρ
P in I Chron. 3:5 (MT vs. 6) and 14:5 ܥܒܢ
which may help to explain;ܥܘܒܪ here. Perhaps
ܥܒܢ; in P at first and then by metathesis
confused ܒ and ܒ, and wrote ;ܥܘܒܪ. V and
T follow Mt.

11:3 אֶל־עַם P ܐܠܝܥܡ Cf. 23:34 where P ܐܠܝܠ
correctly. LXX, confusing ב and ם, 'Ελιάβ
V,T follow MT.

15:27, 36 יְהוֹנָתָן P ܝܘ, using the common abbreviation. LXX ʼΙωναθίν. V and T follow MT.

20:6 אֲבִישַׁ֖י P ܘܠܐܒ LXX[B] Ἀβειισά LXX[A] Ἀβισαεί

V Abisai T اَبِیشَی .

21:14 בְּצֵלְעָ֑ע P ܘܪܡܚ, confusing it with

הַצֵּלָע also in Benjamin, cf. I Sam. 10:2,

LXX πλευρᾷ and V in latere, making it a

common noun. T follows MT. In Josh. 18:28,

the only other occurrence of צֵלָע P ܠܐ .

23:28 חֲלֶ֖ץ הַפְּלֹטִ֑י pL,Le ܐܠܨܝ ܚܠܨ, pA,M,BH ܐܠܘܨܝ ܚܠܨ

cf. v. 29 where Pܐܠܘܨܝ ܚܠܨ, and I Chron. 11:30

ܐܠܘܨܝ. In II Kings 25:23 P ܚܠܨ

while the parallel in Jer. 40:8 has ܐܠܘ ܚܠܨ

LXX[B]ʼΕντωφατείτης LXX[A] Νεττωφα θειτης

V,T follow MT.

23:31 הָעַרְבָתִ֑י P ܥܪܒܬܝ ܚܠ, which may be a case

of interpretation by P. Cf. I Chron. 11:33

ܐܪܒܬܝ 12:3 ܐܥܠܒ 8:36 ܚܪܒܠܐ LXX here

ʼαρβωθ. V Asmaveth and T הָעַרְבָתִ֑י 28

23:35 חֶצְרַ֖י הַכַּרְמְלִ֑י pA ܚܨܪܝ pL,Le,BH ܚܝܢ pM ܚܢ

LXX[A] Φαράει LXX[B]ʼΟυραιοερχεί 29. It is

possible that פ was not transliterated; then

p[A] confused ד and ר , while pL,Le,M trans-

literated ע with ܢ .

23:38 יִתְרָ֑א P ܝܬܪ, as also in parallel in I Chron

11:40. Here λ was transliterated by ܪ. MT is

supported by LXX[B] Γηράβ and LXX[A] Γαρηθ 30.

V Gareb and T בִּרְדָּ֫.

24:5 עֲרוֹעֵר P ܐܠܥܙ. MT is supported by Ἀροηρ

LXX[A]; and LXX[B] Ἀροηλ. V in Aroer T בַּעֲרֹעֵר.

This too may be interpretation by P.

VI. Did P follow Ketib or Qere?

In II Samuel there are 28 cases of Ketib and Qere
in which P shows a preference for one or the other of
the readings. In 22 of these cases, P follows Q; in
the other 6, K.

P follows Q:

1:11 K בְגִדְו Q בְּגָדָיו P ܠܒܘܫܗ

3:15 K אִישָׁהּ Q אִישָׁהּ P ܒܥܠܗ , so 'A.

5:2 K הַיִּיתָה הַמּוֹצִיא וְהַמֵּבִי אֶת־יִשְׂרָאֵל Q הָיִיתָ הַמּוֹצִיא וְהַמֵּבִי
    P ܐܢܬ ܗܘ ܡܦܩ ܘܡܥܠ ܗܘܝܬ

8:3 K בִּנְהַר Q בִּפְרָת P ܦܪܬ ,so about
    45 Mss., LXX and I Chron. 18:3.

10:9 K בְחוּרֵי יִשְׂרָאֵל Q בָּחוּר בְּיִשְׂרָאֵל
    P ܡܢ ܓܒܪܐ ܕܐܝܣܪܐܝܠ so about 50 Mss.

11:1 K הַמַּלְאָכִים Q הַמְּלָכִים P ܡܠܟܐ ,, so
    about 25 Mss., LXX,V,T, I Chron. 20:1

12:20 K שִׂמְלֹתֻו Q שִׂמְלֹתָיו P ܠܒܘܫܗ

12:24 K וַיִּלַּד Q וַתֵּלֶד P ܘܝܠܕܬ so 11 Mss., T.

13:33 K כִּי אִם אַמְנֹון Q אִם P ܐܠܐ

13:37   K רח֑ימעַ Q דוחי֑מעַ P ܝܘܚܢ, so
about 24 Mss., LXX,V,T.

15:28   K בערות Q בְּעַרבֹות P ܟܘܡܪ, so
LXX, V,T.

16:2   K וֹנל֑חֶם Q ונלחֶם P ܘܠܚܡ, so 30 Mss.

16:18   K לֹא Q לֹ֑ו P ܠܗ, so LXX,V,T.

16:23   K בדבר־שֶׁאַל֑ Q inserts אישׁ P ܡܛܠܠܘܕ, ܐܝܟ
so about 30 Mss.

17:16   K בְּעַרבֹות Q בְּעַרבֹות P ܟܘܡܪܐ, so about
48 Mss.

18:13   K בנַפשֹׁו Q בנַפשׁי P ܒܢܦܫܗ, so about
24 Mss., LXX^L.

21:9   K תחלת Q בְּתחלת P ܒܫ

23:20   K חיל Q חַיל P ܚܝܠܐ

23:21   K אַשֶׁר Q אישׁ P ܠܓܒܪܐ, so I Chron. 11:23.

23:35   K חֶצרַי Q חֶצרֹו P ܚܨܪܝ

23:37   K נ֑שֵׁא Q נֹשֵׁא P ܫܩܠ

24:14   K רַחֲמֹיו Q רַחֲמֹו P ܪܚܡܘܗܝ;

P follows K:

3:25   K מֹבֹאֶךָ P מבֹואֶךָ Q ܡܥܠ

12:9   K בְּעֵינֹו Q, so 8 Mss. בְּעֵינֹי P ܐܠܗܐ ܡܪ

14:22   K עַבְדֹו Q, so 15 Mss. עבדֶךָ P ܥܒܕܗ

16:12   K קללתֹו Q, so 71 Mss. קללתֹ P ܨܘܚܝܬܐ

20:23   K הַדְבָרֹי Q, so LXX^A הַדְרֶתֹי P ܚ; ܝ

22:51   K מִגְדֹלֹ Q מִגְדֹל P בב; ܠ, so Ps.18:50,LXX.

Notes

1. *JBL* (1938), 209-213.

2. *Introduction to the Old Testament* (New York, 1941) p. 86

3. *Introduction to the Massorectico-critical Edition of the Hebrew Bible* (London, 1897) pp. 364-365.

4. *Notes on the Hebrew Text and the Topography of the Books of Samuel* (Oxford, 1913) pp. 294-295.

5. *Ibid*., p. 325.

6. *Introduction to the Old Testament in Greek* (Cambridge, 1902) p. 304.

7. Driver, *op. cit*., p. lxiv.

8. Lagarde, *Onomastica*, quotes Jerome "region of the Titans" in 110,25 and "valley or the Allofyloi" in 147,6; also Eusebius Κοιλὰς Τιτάνων in 272,71 and Ραφάειν in 288,22.

9. *Ibid*. as "Nachon" 143,4 and Ναχών 284,26.

10. Driver, *op. cit*., p. 354, note 2.

11. Lagarde, *op. cit*., 37,19 as "Ararites"

12. *Ibid*., 37,20 as "Aradius"

13. *Ibid*., 39,9 as "Iahazaher"

14. *Ibid*., 38,23 as "Gom" and 129,23 as "Gob"; also Γόβ 247,89.

15. Driver, *op. cit*., p. 241, "perhaps correctly."

16. Lagarde, *op. cit*., 166,9 as Θατίρι and 37,3 "Asuri".

Notes

17. _Ibid._, 140,16 "Masbach" and 281,56 Μασβάχ.

18. _Ibid._, 37,19 "Adollam"

19. _Ibid._, 37,23 "Abialbon"

20. _Ibid._, 39,8 as "Iasan"

21. _Ibid._ 38,9 as "Bethoron"

22. _AJSL_ (1912) 274 ff.

23. Lagarde, _op. cit._, 238,87 βαουρείμ ; also 37,26
    as "Beurim" and 107,3 as "Baurim"

24. _Ibid._, 38,2 as "Bethroob"

25. Driver, _op. cit._, p. 364.

26. _Ibid._, p. 370

27. Lagarde, _op. cit._, 293,25 as Σικελάγ.

28. _Ibid._, 37,24 as "Azmath"

29. _Ibid._, 38,21 as "Farai"

30. _Ibid._, 38,24 as "Garab"

Chapter III
THE INFLUENCE OF OTHER TRANSLATIONS

I. The Influence of the Septuagint

AS WE HAVE NOTED in the Introduction, P was strongly
influenced by LXX. This is shown by the many additions
to MT, by the many omissions of MT, and by the modes of
translation which both versions together show. Not
infrequently, these changes, whether additions or omissions or modes of translation, are correct emendations
and when they are so judged, note is taken of such
correction of MT.

P followed LXX in adding to MT:

3:7 ܠܘܩܒܠ, so V, for the sake of clarity. The
Jewish Version inserts the word in brackets.
In 3:11, the word is added for the same reason.
In 4:1, it is added again, this time with V,
correctly. Driver[1] quoted Weir who suggests
that it was omitted because of the resemblance
of אשׁ בעל to ושׁמע׳ל preceding.

3:8 אחמר ܐܚܡܪ

3:13 וم°ץ

3:15 אישׁ P ܚܠܘܬ LXX ἀνδρὸς αὐτῆς   V a viro
suo T בַּעְלָהּ. This is a correct emendation.

3:20 וֹתְחָבְּרִין P ܘܐܫܡܒ°ץ 8 Mss.   פְּתַחְבְּרִין

4:2 ܒܢ̈ܝ[2*]

5:1 ܠܗ, so 8 Mss.

5:4 אַרְבָּעִים P ܘܐܪ̈ܒܥܝܢ, so 14 Mss., V, correctly.

5:6 הַמְּצֻדָה. I Chron. 11:4, LXX דָּוִד P ܕܘܝܕ ܡܠܟܐ

5:23 ܛܘܪܐ for the sake of clarity

6:6 ܐܝܕܗ, so I Chron. 13:9, V T, correctly.

9:2 ܐܢܐ, so V.

11:6 P ܠܗ ܘܐܡܪ LXX λέγων V dicens

12:1 ܒܥܡܐ, so 3 Mss.

12:22 ܕܘܝܕ

13:32 ܡܠܟܐ

13:37 ܕܘܝܕ

14:30 ܐܘܩܕܘܗ̇

15:21 ܬܡܢ, so Σ, Θ.

16:10 ܫܒܘܩܘܗܝ

17:28 ܩܠܝܬܐ ܘܩܡܚܐ, correctly. LXX read עשׁרת

18:14 ܠܘܬܗ

18:23 ܐܡܪ ܠܗ, correctly[2]

18:26 ܐܚܪܢܐ, so V, correctly[3]

19:5 (P v. 4) ܘܐܡܪ but P^{ES} follows MT.

19:10 (P v. 9) ܕܠܗܘܢ

19:15 (P v. 14) ܘܐܡܪܘ ܠܗ

19:27 (P v. 26) ܡܫܡܫܢܟ

19:43 (P v. 42) ܘܐܡܪܘ

20:16 ܘܐܡܪܬ

23:20 מֵיטִב גְּאוֹנֵי אֲנָשִׁים סׁ P inserts בְּיַד correctly.[4]

P followed LXX in omissions of MT:

1:4 וַיָּמֻתוּ

2:15 וּלְאִישׁ־בַּיּ דָּשָׁה P>ו correctly[5]

3:36 כְּלֹי P, LXX, V > כִּי

3:38 וְגָדוֹל P > וְ

4:11 הַלֹּיא

7:5 אֶל־[2] P> so 19 Mss. and V.

7:8 לְדָוִיד P > לְ so 5 Mss.

7:11 וָפֶּקֶן P > וְ

7:23 כְּיִשְׂרָאֵל P > כִּ so 9 Mss.

8:10 הֵעִי[2]

9:10 דָּיָה!

14:25 יְפֶה

17:28 וְקָלִי[2] correctly[6].

20:14 אַף correctly[7]

23:13 רֹאשׁ correctly[8]

23:20 בֶּן[2] correctly[9]

23:25 אֱלִיקָא הַחֲרֹדִי with LXX[B] and I Chron.11:27

24:23 וָפִסְדָּך

P followed LXX in translation

1:9 הַחֹשֶׁךְ ? P ‖ ;ـ٥٤ LXX σκότος δεινὸν

2:27 וַיֶּאֱסֹ֥ף יוֹם P ‖ ﺟﺒ LXX κύριος

Driver[10] as always elsewhere.

3:18 וַיֹּשִׁיעַ Pﺣﺰ٥ق/LXX σῶσαι 35 Mss.

אוֹשִׁיעַ Driver[11] quotes Keil,"a clerical error".

3:24-25   הָעֵין׀   P in v. 25 ⊓   LXX in v.25 οὐκ

5:8   בַּצִּנּוֹר   P ܣܟܡܐ "with a shield", reading בַּצִּנָּה or inner Syriac error for ܣܟܡܐ "in the gutter"   LXX παραξιφίδι.

6:1   וַיֹּסֶף   P ܘܟܢܫ LXX συνήγαγεν ,correctly.[12]

6:2   שֵׁם שֵׁם   P ܬܡܢ ܒܠ LXX ⊰ שֵׁם 30 Mss. שֵׁם שֵׁם

7:5   הַאַתָּה   P ⊔ LXX οὐ I Chron. 17:4 לֹא

7:15   יָסוּר   P ܐܥܒܪ LXX ἀποστήσω I Chron.17:13 אָסִיר

7:15   מִלְּפָנֶיךָ   P ܩܕܡܝ LXX μου

7:16   לְפָנֶיךָ   P ܩܕܡܝ LXX ἐμοῦ

7:23   הָלְכוּ   P ⊔ܘܢ LXX ὡδήγησεν correctly[13].

8:12   מֵאֲרָם   P ܡܢ ܐܕܘܡ LXX ἐκ τῆς Ἰδουμαίας correctly[14] so 9 Mss.

9:11   שֻׁלְחָנִי   P ܦܬܘܪܗ ܕܡܠܟܐ LXX[BA] Δαυειδ LXX[L] βασιλεως.

11:12   מִמָּחֳרָת: וַיֵּשֶׁב דָּוִד בִּירוּשָׁלַ‍ P ܦܫ ܘܢܐ ܒܐܘܪܫܠܡ ܘܒܝܘܡܐ ܐܚܪܢܐ so LXX[L].

12:9   MT[Q] בְּעֵינַי   MT[K] בְּעֵינָיו P ܩܕܡܝ LXX αὐτοῦ

13:19   יָדָהּ   P ܐܝܕܝܗ LXX τὰς χεῖρας αὐτῆς

14:4   וַתָּבֹא   P ܘܥܠܬ LXX εἰσῆλθεν so V T, mlt. Mss., correctly[15].

15:7   אַרְבָּעִים   P ܐܪܒܥ LXX[L] τέσσαρα correctly[16].

15:8   בְּשַׁבְתִּי   P ܐܢ ܐܗܦܟ LXX ἐπιστρέφων correctly[17].

15:19   לְמִמָּקוֹם P ܡܢ ܐܬܪ LXX ἐκ   correctly[18].

15:31 הַגִּיד הֵן! P ܪܝܘ ܟܘܘܘ LXX ἀνηγγέλη
     correctly.[19]

15:35 וְלֹבִיא) P ܠܝ / ܐܢ LXX καὶ ἰδοὺ

16: 12 MT[K] וּבְרֶנְי MT[Q] בְּרֶנְי P ܚܡܪ ܚܣܘ [20].
     Correctly.[21]

16:15 אִישׁ הָעָם־כָּל! LXX[B] πᾶς ἀνήρ LXX[A] πᾶς ὁ λαὸς
     P ܠܒܢ ܘܟܠܘ correctly?[22]

16:18 MT[K] לֹא MT[Q] לֹי P ܘܠ LXX αὐτῷ correctly[23]

17:5 קְרָא P ܩܪܘ LXX καλέσατε correctly[24]

17:13 אֹתֹו P ܐܘܬܘ נְתַּי!LXX αὐτὴν, so V,T.

17:24 בָּא P ܐܬܐ LXX διῆλθεν

17:28 וְסֹפֵים! P ܐܠ ܐܠܘ LXX ἀμφιτάπους

18:9 וְבְּד! P ܠܠܠܘ LXX ἐκρεμάσθη   so T

23:13 וֶשְׁשִׁים P ܐܠܠ LXX τρεῖς   correctly?[30]

24:4 זְפֵר! P ܒ ܪ ܛ, so LXX[L], V.

    Thus it can be seen that of the 33 additions to
MT, which P and LXX made, 8 were made correctly, while
several others can be said to be necessary for the sake
of clarity.

    Of the 17 omissions of MT by P and LXX, 5 can be
said to be correct.

    Of the 51 cases in which P follows LXX in mode of
translation over against MT, 20 are considered correct.

    We notice also that in six cases, P agrees with
the Lucianic recension. In one case, P goes with Σ, θ.

12 examples have support from the Mss.

In 8 cases, V also agrees with LXX and P.

In 5 cases, T also agrees with LXX and P.

Besides these cases, there are 4 examples of proper names which were influenced by LXX. They are dealt with in the section on proper names.

II. The Influence of the Targum

Driver[31] finds that the influence of the Targum is not as great in the books of Samuel as in the Pentateuch It is nevertheless present and may be traced in certain characteristic expressions which would hardly be met with beyond the reach of Jewish influence. Expressions such as "to say, speak, worship, pray, sin before God", where the Hebrew has simply "to God", a distinctive feature of the exegesis embodied in the Targums, are met with similarly in the Peshitto of Samuel.

The examples of such influence follows:

Ref	P (Syriac/Hebrew)		T (Syriac/Hebrew)
1:24	עֲדָנִ֑ים	P ܨܒ̈ܬܐ	T עֲדָינִ֑ים
3:19	בְּאָזְנֵי	P ܩܕܡ	T קֳדָם
3:28	עִם	P ܩܕܡ ܡܢ	T קֳדָם מִן
5:6	וַיֹּ֫אמֶר	P ܘܐܡܪ̈ܘ	T וַאֲמַר֫וּ
6:9	אֶת־יְהֹוָה	P ܩܕܡ ܡܢ	T מִן קֳדָם
6:14	מְכַרְכֵּ֥ר	P ܡܫܒܚ	T מְשַׁבַּח
6:16	מְפַזֵּ֫ז וּמְכַרְכֵּ֥ר	P ܘܡܫܒܚ ܘܪܡܙ	
	T מְרַקֵּד וּמְשַׁבַּח		

7:10   לְיִשְׂרָאֵל   P,T > לְ

7:15   P מִשְׁפָּעֵם...   ܠ ܡܢ ܛܡ
       T   מִן קָדָ֑ם

7:27   אֵלָ֗יה   P ܡܢ ܛܡ   T קָדָ֑ךְ

8:18   סְעָדִים   P ܙ ܢ ܣ ܚ   T רַבְרְבִין

11:23 וַזְהִירָה   P ܡܣܬ‌ܠܠ   T וְהַוָּא שַׁרְדִין

11:27 בְּעֵינַי   P ܡܢ ܠ   T קָדָ֑ם

12:5   בֶּן־מָוֶת   P ܘ ܡܣܕ   T חַיָּב קְטוֹל

12:13 לַיהוה   P ܡܢ ܠ   T קָדָ֑ם

12:21 בְּעָבוּר   P ܚܢ   T עַל

12:27 וָעַ֫יִם   P ܘܛܠܚܡ‌ܠ   T פִלְכוּתָא

13:14 אֵמֶ֫ת   P ܣܛܚܢ   T קְשׁוֹט

14:33 לִפְנֵי־הַמֶּלֶךְ P ܡܢ ܠ   T קָדָ֑ם

15:2,6 לָבוֹא אֶשְׁפָּ֖ט וַיֻּרֵד לַמִּשְׁפָּט
       P ܛܠܚܢ ܡܢ ܠ T וְדֵן אָצֵא לָבוֹא קָדֶ֫ם

17:13 וְנִמְצָא   P ܣܒܣܡ   T וְשָׁאַר

17:29 בְּקָר שִׁפוֹת P ܙ‌ܠ‌ܘ, ܣ ܟܘ
       T וְגִבְּדִין דַּחֲלַב חוֹרִין

18:8   וַיֻּרֵב   P+ ܠ‌ܐܝܢ   T+ חֻ֫יַּם

18:12 בָּאָזְנֵ֑יו   P ܡܢ ܛܡ   T קָדָ֑מָא אֵן

18:22 בְּנָ֫פֶשׁ   P ܣ ܚ   T מֵן דַּהֲב

21:6   לַיהוה   P ܡܢ ܠ   T קָדָ֑ם

21:10 וָזַם   P ܣ‌ܠܢܣ   T דְּנַחֲת

23:14 וַיֻּמֵ֫ץ   P ܚܢ ܣ ܙ ܣ ܟ   T וְאַסְרְטִין

23:16 לַיהוה   P ܡܢ ܠ   T קָדָ֑ם

23:17	יְהוָה	P	ܡܪܝܐ	T	קְדָם	מִן
24:4	לִפְנֵי	P	ܡܪܝܐ	T	קְדָם	
24:10	אֶל-יְהוָה	P	ܡܪܝܐ	T	קְדָם	
24:13	צָרֶיךָ	P	ܚܣܟ ܠܟ	T	פְּאֵיךָ	
24:17	אֶל-יְהוָה	P	ܡܪܝܐ	T	קְדָם	

III. Agreement with the Vulgate

There were a number of cases in which V and P go together against MT. They are as follows:

3:29	בַּפֶּלֶךְ	P ܟܛܠܡܐ	V fusum, so 'A, Є.
6:19	וְאֶשְׁפָּר	P ܘܚܣܡ	

      V assaturam bubulae carnis

9:1	יֶשׁ-עוֹד	P ܠܟ ܐܝܬ	V est aliquis
11:23	עַד-פֶּתַח הַשָּׁעַר	P ܥܠ ܬܪܥܐ	

      V ad portam civitatis

13:20	וַיּוֹן	P ܛܒܝ	V concubuit
13:32	אַל-יֹאמַר	P ܣܒܪ ܠܐ	V ne aestimet
14:20	וְלַדַּבֵּר	P ܗܕܐ	V istud
16:8	בְּרָעָתֶךָ	P ܐܝܠܝܢ ܕܒܝܫܢ	V premunt te mala
17:22	נֶעְדָּר	P ܚܕ	V residuus fuit
18:14	בְּלֵב	P ܒܠܒܐ	V haerens
19:39 (P v. 38)	הַזֶּה בָּחַר	P ܘܒܥܝܬ	V petieris
20:2	וַיַּעַל	P ܘܦܪܩ	V separatus est.... a David
23:3	צוּר	P ܡܫܝܚܐ	V fortis

Notes

1.   Driver, op. cit., p. 252

2.   Ibid., p. 331, "as the Hebrew idiom requires"

3.   Ibid., p. 331

4.   Ibid., p. 368.

5.   Ibid., p. 242

6.   Ibid., p. 327

7.   Ibid., p. 345

8.   Ibid., p. 366

9.   Ibid., p. 368

10.   Ibid., p. 244

11.   Ibid., p. 249

12.   Ibid., p. 265

13.   Ibid., pp. 271-278.

14.   Ibid., p. 282

15.   Ibid., p. 306

16.   Ibid., p. 311

17.   Ibid., p. 311

18.   Ibid., p. 313, "a copyist's error"

19.   Ibid., p. 316

20.   Ginsburg, op. cit., p. 355, thinks the original
      text was בְּעֵינָיו but was changed to avoid an-
      thropomorphism.

21.   Driver, op. cit., p. 319.

22.   Ibid., p. 319, thinks that אִישׁ came into the text
      by an error from the line above.

23. *Ibid.*, p. 319

24. *Ibid.*, p. 321

25. *Ibid.*, p. 332

26. *Ibid.*, p. 334

27. *Ibid.*, p. 336

28. *Ibid.*, p. 337

29. *Ibid.*, p. 354 thinks this a corruption of the name of a rare weapon which the Philistine used.

30. *Ibid.*, p. 365.

Chapter IV

CONCLUSION

THERE ARE PROBLEMS presented by the Peshitto that still remain partly unsolved: particularly those questions dealing with the authorship and origin. Strictly speaking, the Peshitto was not the work of a single translator but was produced at various times by translators whose ideals were not exactly alike. Heller[1], however, claims that the Peshitto is the work of one author, although he admits the possibility of another author's being responsible for Chronicles. On the other hand, internal evidence that several translators produced it may be found in the varying standards of excellence which appear in different books or groups of books.

For example, it seems that the Pentateuch was translated first. This can be seen from the fact that passages from it found in later biblical books are practically quoted from the Syriac Pentateuch and unlike the Book of Psalms which is a free translation influenced by LXX[2], the Pentateuch is a literal version.

Ezekiel and Proverbs closely resemble the Targums[3]. The minor prophets are, for the most part, well although freely translated, and exhibit LXX influence[4] as does also the book of Isaiah.[5] The text of Job, although a close translation, is in parts unintelligible, due partly

to corruptions from external causes and probably through
the influence of other translations.[6] The Song of Songs
is a literal translation; Ruth is a paraphrastic version,
while Chronicles is also paraphrastic and contains
Midrashic elements.

Thus there is abundant evidence of the plurality of
authorship of the Peshitto. The precise number is of
no particular importance, nor could it, in the present
state of our knowledge, be definitely ascertained.
Roediger[7], was therefore right in his assertion that
"it is necessary to accept as certainty that in the
translation of the Old Testament several translators
had part; for quite often it makes an entirely different
impression in the different books."

The next question that arises is "Who were the translators of the Peshitto? Were they Jews or Christians
or Judaeo-Christians?" Those who credit with some
historical value the Syrian tradition which places the
origin of the Peshitto in the time of Abgar are inclined
to think that the Peshitto is solely the work of Christian authorship. Among these we may mention the Gaon
Samuel b. Hofni, Hirzel, Kirsch, DeWette, Keil, Gottheil
Margolis, and others.[8]

Their argument is that from the earliest time of
which we have available information, the Peshitto has

been claimed by the Christians of the various Syrian

Churches as their version and they have used it from

the end of the 4th Century down to our own day. Buhl[9]

and Nöldeke[10] maintain that the Syrian Christians in

Palestine have another version in their own dialect,

made very likely from the Greek. This view goes back

to Bar Hebraeus who divides the Syrians into eastern

and western and speaks of the two Syriac versions of

the Bible, one the Peshitto made from the Hebrew, and

the other, a paraphrastic rendering from the Greek.

The internal evidence of the Peshitto goes to prove

that it must have proceeded from Christian hands.

Rather strong is the evidence adduced in favor of

Christian authorship of the Peshitto derived from the

air of negligence apparent in the rendering of the

Levitical laws, particularly in the sections concerning

clean and unclean animals, which would scarcely have

proceeded from Jewish hands.

More decisive, perhaps, are the arguments adduced

by the interpretation of the many passages which lend

themselves to Christian coloring. For example, the

word עַלְמָה in Isaiah 7:14 is given as ‎ܒܬܘܠܬܐ

in the Peshitto to make it conform to the New Testament

quotation in Matt. 1:23. Other passages where Christian

influence is traceable are: Is. 9:2; 52:15; 53:8; Jer.

31:31; Hos. 13:14 and Zech. 12:10.

These and similar quotations would furnish quite
reliable proof of Christian authorship, provided we
could be certain that they were part of the original
version and not due to subsequent modification. This
however cannot be demonstrated and therefore we cannot
possibly assert with any definiteness that the Peshitto
of the Old Testament is the work of Christian authorship.[11]

On the other hand, Kahle in a recent work[12] holds
to the view that the Peshitto has to be regarded as the
work of a Jewish translator, made for the use of a
Jewish community. Such a community he finds in Adia-
bene, a kingdom situated between the two rivers Zab,
to the east of the river Tigris, which formed a part of
the great Parthian Empire.

Bloch[13] is another of those who venture the opinion
that the Peshitto is a product of the early efforts by
the Aramaic-speaking Jews to bring out a vernacular
rendering of the Bible, to supplement, but not to re-
place, the original Hebrew text. He quotes Buhl[14],
"The very fact that the translation attached itself to
the Hebrew text shows that it owed its existence to
Jewish labors, which is further confirmed by the sympath
shown in it for the traditional Scripture exposition of

the Jews". Besides there are those scholars who maintain
that the influence of the Targum is strongly felt in
some books.[15] Perles noticed it in the Pentateuch,
especially in Genesis, Cornill[16] in Ezekiel, and
Fränkel in Chronicles[17].

As further proof, Bloch[18] mentions II Sam. 24:15, a
passage in which the Peshitto diverges from the Massoretic text and in so doing follows the interpretation
of the Targum. He also quotes II Kings 25:3; also the
fact that the tetragrammaton is always translated by
the Peshitto as ܡܪܝܐ , which is in accord with the
rabbinic tradition to read יהוה as if it were אדני.
That the Apocrypha were originally wanting in the Syriac
Bible is another proof of the Jewish character of the
translation.

The conjecture that it is a work of Judaeo-Christians
is advanced, no doubt, with a view to compromising the
two diametrically opposed views which favor either
Jewish or Christian authorship. Nöldeke[19], who considers
the Peshitto a Christian work, finds evidence of Jewish
help in its execution. In I Chron. 5:2 the passage
"for Judah prevailed above his brethren and of him
came the prince נגיד "is rendered in the Peshitto
"from Judah shall come forth the King Messiah".

Buhl[20] maintains that "the probability is strongly

in favor of the view that it owes its origins to Christian effort, while, to some extent, fragments of other
Jewish translations have been made use of in it; and
for the rest, the translation was made by Jewish-
Christians." Under the circumstances, it is impossible
to prove or disprove the theory, since we have no means
of definitely discriminating between the Jewish and the
Christian elements.

If we consider the Syriac translation as a whole to
be a Christian work, we shall have to assume the foundin
of the Christian Church in that region about 150 C.E. as
the termimus a quo of its origin. The first certain
witness we have for its existence is given by Aphraates
about 200 years later; but without any doubt, seeing
that the Greek had not spread in that eastern region,
a translation of the Holy Scriptures into the language
of the people would, very soon after the founding of
the Church in that land, be felt a necessity.

At a later period, a large portion of the Syrians,
with little reason, abandoned their old independent
translation through admiration for the over-estimated
LXX. The chief leader in this movement was Theodore
of Mopsuestia, who repeatedly reproaches those who
esteemed more highly an unknown translator (ἕνα τινὰ
ἀφανῆ   ) than the seventy-two inspired translators

Yet even in the following generations, when the Syrian language ceased to be spoken, the Peshitto was preserved by the Jacobites as well as by the Nestorians.

Although the Peshitto attaches itself to the original text, it still shows here and there, especially in some books, a sort of similarity to the LXX, so that a dependence in that direction must be assumed. But how far the agreement is capable of explanation by the supposition that the translators during their work may have used the LXX, or that it had been occasioned only by later revisions according to the Alexandrine translation, has not been as yet determined and will probably always remain doubtful. The similarity with the LXX is in all essential respects equally strong in all, even the oldest, manuscripts and in the quotations of Aphraates, so that such a recasting must in any case have taken place at a very early date.

The striking agreement between many variants of the Peshitto and LXX from the MT has long been recognized. It was noticed and commented upon by Perles[21], Ryssel[22], Cornill[23], and many others. Barnes[24] points out that "the influence of the LXX frequently takes effect on the ideas or on the manner of the Syriac translators rather than on their words". Assuming that "it seems tolerably certain that alterations were made from time

to time with a view to harmonizing the Syriac text with
that of LXX"[25], we must reckon with another difficulty,
namely, the condition of the LXX text. As the active
influence of the Greek over the Syriac lasted, it seems,
for a period extending over several centuries, the Greek
itself underwent considerable change. Sometimes the
hand laid on the Peshitto is that of the unrevised LXX,
sometimes it is the hand of Theodotion or Symmachus,
acting through the Hexaplar text. The Greek Bible in
almost any form seems to have carried weight with the
Syrians.

The mutual relation of the versions has an important
bearing on their value as witnesses and subsequently
the presence or absence of interdependence must be established more or less regularly. Merx[26] has laid down
the following rules; each, however, is subject to ex-
ceptions:

1. If the LXX and Peshitto agree against the
   MT, they comprise the older text.
2. If the Peshitto and MT agree against the
   LXX, then it is possible, but not probable,
   that the latter has the true text.
3. If the MT and LXX agree against the Peshitto,
   then only the weightiest inner reasons can
   sway the decision in favor of the Peshitto.

These are substantially the rules now generally
followed. It is not enough to discern traces of Greek
influence in the rendering of individual words. It
must be determined, if possible, how that influence was

brought to bear on the text: whether the LXX was an
auxiliary to the translator of the Syriac text or whether
there was a still greater dependence: the translator
using the Greek as a language more familiar to him than
the Hebrew. It may be that the readings of both LXX
and Peshitto, when they agree, go back to the pre-
massoretic Hebrew text.[27]

That there exists a possible relation between the
LXX and the Peshitto as a whole, one cannot doubt. But
to determine the possible relationship is not so simple
a matter. First, one must examine the two texts and
collate the cases where the LXX and Peshitto agree over
against MT. Then one must bear in mind the later
editorial efforts to bring the Greek and Syriac text
of the Bible in harmony with one another. The problem
of the dependency of the versions as a whole is very
complicated and Margolis[28] is right in his assertion
that "no single method will do justice to the problem."

It is evident that the Peshitto of Second Samuel
tends more to the school of freedom in translation than
to the extreme of literalness. It has been influenced
to a great extent by the LXX and to a less extent by
the Targum. When it was written and by whom it is impossible in our present state of knowledge to say. My
own feeling is that it may well have been done by Jewish

translators.

Notes

1. C. Heller, <u>Untersuchungen</u> über <u>die Peschitta</u> zur <u>gesamten hebräischen Bibel</u> (Berlin, 1911), p. 3 ff. Cf. Nöldeke <u>Die Alttestamentliche Literatur in einer Reihe von Aufsatzen dargestellt</u> (Leipzig, 1868), p. 264.

2. Berg, <u>op. cit.</u>

3. J. Perles <u>Meletemata Peschitthoniana</u> (Vratislaviae, 1859), p. 14.

4. Berg, <u>op. cit.</u> and M. Bebök, <u>op. cit.</u>

5. W. Barnes in <u>Journal of Theological Studies</u>, II, (1901), 186-197.

6. Stenij, <u>op. cit.</u>

7. In Ersch and Gruber <u>Allgemeine Encyklopedia</u> (Leipzig, 1845), article "Peschito", sec. 3, XVIII, col. 292a-294a, "So ist es für gewiss anzunehmen dass an der Übertragung des alten Testaments mehrere Übersetzer Theil haben, denn sie macht in den verschiedenen Büchern nicht selten einen ganz verschiedenen Eindruck."

8. Perles, <u>op. cit.</u>, p. 21. Nöldeke, <u>op. cit.</u>, p. 263.

9. F. Buhl, <u>Canon and Text of the Old Testament</u> (Edinburgh, 1892), p. 186.

10. Nöldeke, <u>op. cit.</u>, p. 265.

11. cf. Wiseman <u>Horae Syriacae</u> (Roma, 1828), p. 100 ff.

12. P. Kahle The Cairo Geniza (London, 1947), pp. 179-197.

13. J. Bloch in AJSL, 35 (1919), 215-222.

14. Buhl, op. cit., p. 185 ff.

15. A. Mingana in JQR, N.S., VI (1915-1916), 387 ff.

16. C. Cornill op. cit., p. 154 ff.

17. Fränkel op. cit., 508 ff. and 720 fr.

18. Bloch, op. cit., 221.

19. Nöldeke, op. cit., p. 263 ff.

20. Buhl, op. cit., p. 186.

21. Perles, op. cit., p. 4.

22. V. Ryssel, Untersuchungen über die Textgestalt und die Echtheit des Buches Micha (Leipzig, 1887), p. 169.

23. Cornill, op. cit., p. 153 ff.

24. Barnes, op. cit., 186 ff.

25. W. Wright A Short History of Syriac Literature (London, 1894), p. 4.

26. Merx Das Gedicht von Hiob, p. lxxiii, "Stimmt Peschita und Septuaginta gegen den massoretischen Text, so enthalten sie das Ältere. Stimmt Peschita und Masora gegen Septuaginta, so hat letztere das Präjudiz, aber nicht die Gewissheit, das Echte zu bieten. Stimmt Masora und Septuaginta gegen Peschita, so können nur die gewichtigsten innern Gründe die Entscheidung auf die Seite der Peschita

lenken."

27. Cf. J. Reider in <u>JQ</u>R, VII, (1917) 287 ff. with
    reference to the Septuagint and the minor Greek
    versions.

28. Margolis in <u>JQ</u>R, III (1912-1913), 132.

APPENDIX

The Parallels between II Samuel 22 and Psalm 18

There are 59 variants between the MT of II Samuel 22 and the MT of Psalm 18. Of these 59, P in II Sam. has been made to conform to the P of Psalms in 55 cases.

Vs. 1 יָּדַף Ps. מְיַד P | ܒܐܝܕ | ܘܡܢ

Vs. 2 Ps.+ חִזְקִי יהוה אֶרְחָמְךָ P+ ܘܐܡܪ ܪܚܡܟ ܡܪܝܐ ܚܝܠܝ

Vs. 5 מִשְׁבְּרֵי Ps. חֶבְלֵי P ܚܒܠܐ so LXX.

Vs. 7 אֶקְרָא Ps. אֲשַׁוַּע P ܐܩܥܐ so LXX.

Ps.+ קוֹלִי P+ ܩܠܝ

Vs. 8 הַשָּׁמַיִם Ps. הָרִים P | ܛܘܪܐ |

Vs. 11 וַיֵּרָא Ps. וַיֵּדֶא P ܘܛܣ

Vs. 12 Ps.+ סָבִיבֹתָיו P+ ܚܕܪܘܗܝ so LXX.

סֻכּוֹת Ps. סֻכָּתוֹ P ܡܛܠܬܗ so LXX. ἡ σκηνὴ αὐτοῦ.

חַשְׁרַת Ps. חֶשְׁכַת P ܚܫܘܟܐ so LXX.

Vs. 13 בָּעֲרוּ Ps. עָבְרוּ P ܥܒܪ (a corruption of ܚܫܟ)

Ps.+ בָּרָד P+ ܘ ܒܪܕܐ

Vs. 14 יַרְעֵם Ps.+ ל P+ ܘ

בַּשָּׁמַיִם Ps. בַּשָּׁמַיִם P ܒܫܡܝܐ

Ps.+ בָּרָד וְגַחֲלֵי אֵשׁ from vs. 13; P+ ܘܒܪܕܐ ܘܓܘܡܪܐ ܕܢܘܪܐ

Vs. 15 חִצִּים Ps. חִצָּיו P ܓܐܪܘܗܝ

רָב Ps. רָב וּבְרָקִים P ܘܒܪܩܐ ܣܓܝܐܐ

so LXX^L ἤστραψεν ἀστραπήν.

MT^Q וֹ(רֹם) MT^K and Ps. הֹמֹ(רֹ)ם P ܪܘܡ

so LXX.

Vs. 16   יַם Ps. פַיִם P قلم ,

.יַגֹל Ps. + וֹ   P+o so LXX.

אֶצְרָךָ יהוה Ps.בְּצָרָת יהוה

P ܠ ܚܝܠ ܠ ܝܚ ܟ

וֹאֶפֹ Ps.אַפֶּךָ   P ܝ ܐ ܠ ܘ

Vs. 18   שָׁאַי Ps. + וֹ   P + o

Vs. 23   MT^K מִשְׁפָּטָו MT^Q and Ps. וֹמִשְׁפָּטָי P ܢܒܚܣ ,

so LXX.

אַסִיר מִצָּר P אַסִיר עָצֹר Ps. ܐܚܙܗ ܛܒ ܘܒܚ ܐ ,

Vs. 25   כִּבֹרָ דָּי P בֹּר כְּדֵי Ps. ܪܨܐ ܘ ,ܐܪܝ

so LXX.

Vs. 26   גֹּבֹר בֹּר Ps. גֹּבֹר P ܠ ܪ so LXX.

Vs. 28   וֹאֵת Ps.אֵת־בְּ כִּי P ܐܠ , ܛ ܠ ܛ

וֹעֵינֶיךָ Ps. עֵינֵיו P ܣܢܬ

so LXX.

Vs. 29   אַמֵּ זָרִי Ps. אָמֵר זָ ר P ܢܝܡ , ܐܠܘ ܠܘ

וֹיהוה Ps. אֱלֹהָי   P , ܐܠܠ

Vs. 30   בְּאֵלֹה Ps.+ו P+o   so LXX.

Vs. 33   מַעֲצֹד וֹ Ps. מְעַזְּרֵ P ܘܣܘ܂ ,

וֹ(נֵ)ר Ps. אָ(רֵ)ן P ܘܣܘ ܒ

MT^K דַּרְכּוֹ MT^Q and Ps. דַּרְכִּי P ܘܐܘܪܚܝ
so LXX.

Vs. 34 MT^K רַגְלָיו MT^Q and Ps. רַגְלַי P ܪ̈ܓܠܝ
so LXX.

Vs. 36 Ps. + וִימִינְךָ תִסְעָדֵנִי + P + ܘܝܡܝܢܟ ܠܣܥܕܢܝ

Vs. 38 וָאַשְׁמִידֵם Ps. וְאַשִּׂיגֵם P ܘܐܕܪܟ ܐܢܘܢ

Vs. 39 Ps. > וָאֲכַלֵּם P > so LXX.

וְלֹא יְכֻלוּן קוּם Ps. יְקוּמוּן
P ܘܠܐ ܢܩܘܡܘܢ

Vs. 41 מְשַׂנְאַי וָאַצְמִיתֵם Ps. וּמְשַׂנְאַי אַצְמִיתֵם
P ܘܠܣܢܐܝ - ܐܘܒܕܬ ܐܢܘܢ

Vs. 42 יִשְׁעוּ Ps. יְשַׁוְּעוּ P ܢܩܥܘܢ so LXX.

Vs. 43 כַּעֲפַר־אֶרֶץ Ps. כְּעָפָר עַל־פְּנֵי רוּחַ
P ܐܝܟ ܥܦܪܐ ܥܠ ܐܦܝ ܪܘܚܐ

אֲדִקֵּם אֶרְקָעֵם Ps. אֲרִיקֵם P ܐܪܘܩ ܐܢܘܢ
so LXX.

Vs. 44 וַתְּפַלְּטֵנִי Ps. and P > ו

עַמִּי Ps. עַם P ܥܡܐ, so LXX.

תִּשְׁמְרֵנִי Ps. תְּשִׂימֵנִי P ܠܪܝܫ ܥ

Vs. 45 b לִשְׁמוֹעַ אֹזֶן יִשָּׁמְעוּ לִי b

a בְּנֵי נֵכָר יִתְכַּחֲשׁוּ־לִי a

Ps. and P invert b and a.

Vs. 46 וְיַחְגְּרוּ Ps. וְיַחְרְגוּ P ܘܢܬܬܙܝܥܘܢ
so LXX.

Vs. 47 צוּרִי Ps. and P >

Vs. 48 וּמ(וֹ)רִיד   Ps. וַיַּדְבֵּר   P ܣܚܡ

so LXX.

Vs. 49 וּמ(וֹ)צִיאִי   Ps. מְפַלְּטִי   P ܛܦ ܣܥ

מֵאֹיְבַי   Ps. and P. + אַף

Vs. 50 בַּגּוֹיִם יהוה   Ps. and P. invert order.

Vs. 51 MT^Q מַגְדִּיל   MT^K and Ps. מִגְדֹּל

P ܒ ; ܠ   so LXX.

The 4 cases in P in II Sam. was not made to conform with the P of Ps. 18 follow:

Vs. 5   כִּי   Ps. >   but P ܠܠܦܠ   so LXX.

Vs. 12   וַשְׁרַת   Ps. >)   but P ܘ   so LXX.

Vs. 39   וָאֲכַלֵּם   Ps. >)   but P ܘ   so LXX.

Vs. 49   הֶחָמָסִים   Ps. חָמָס   but P ܚܣ

so LXX.

It can thus be seen that of these four, two are
the omission of the conjunction וּ while one is the omission of the conjunction כִּי and the other is the
difference between singular and plural.

It is very likely that Psalms was one of the first
OT books to be translated into Syriac and that, when
II Samuel was translated, the Syriac of II Samuel was
made to conform with that of Psalms.

INDEX OF BIBLICAL PASSAGES

18:26	32, 70	20:15	25, 48
18:28	26	20:16	25, 70
18:29	16, 23	20:17	31
19:1	30, 46	20:18	24, 48
19:3	30	20:19	22, 31, 48
19:5	30, 70	20:21	25, 30, 48, 60
19:6	30	20:22	12, 23, 60
19:7	30, 31	20:23	66
19:8	33	20:24	58
19:10	16, 70	20:25	59
19:11	25, 26	20:26	17, 60
19:12	28	21:2	26
19:13	13, 26	21:4	12, 24
19:15	33, 70	21:5	12
19:17	14, 30	21:6	31, 56, 75
19:18	26, 30	21:8	16, 59
19:19	25	21:9	66
19:20	23, 33	21:10	75
19:21	31	21:12	24
19:25	23, 24, 32, 46	21:14	64
19:26	32	21:15	49
19:27	23, 30, 70	21:17	31
19:28	46	21:18	59
19:29	46	21:19	25, 56, 61
19:30	46	21:22	49
19:31	24	22:1	31, 92
19:32	46	22:2	57, 92
19:35	31	22:4	32
19:36	14, 34	22:5	92, 95
19:37	23, 34	22:7	92
19:38	24, 26	22:8	92
19:39	76	22:11	92
19:40	25	22:12	92, 95
19:42	12, 24, 30, 33	22:13	92
19:43	24, 25, 33, 70	22:14	92
19:44	25, 31, 33	22:15	92
20:1	25, 26, 29, 60	22:16	93
20:2	26, 33, 60, 76	22:18	93
20:3	47	22:23	93
20:4	33	22:25	93
20:5	23	22:26	93
20:6	26, 47, 60, 64	22:28	93
20:7	47, 60	22:29	93
20:8	22, 26, 31, 47	22:30	93
20:9	48	22:33	93
20:10	34, 47, 48, 60	22:34	12, 94
20:11	. 26, 32	22:36	12, 13, 94
20:12	26, 48	22:38	94
20:13	26, 47, 60	22:39	94, 95
20:14	12, 32, 71	22:41	94